Rochelle Owens

Luca: Discourse on Life and Death

Intoduction by
Marjorie Perloff

Junction Press
San Diego
2001

Parts of this book have appeared in the journals *Abacus, Another Chicago Magazine, Anabasis, The Cafe Review, Caprice, Confrontation, Contact II, Cover Arts, First Intensity, Paradox, Poetry New York, Postmodern Culture, Talisman, Texture, Backwoods Broadsides,* and *Sulfur,* the anthology *Joy Praise* (Encinitas: Ta'Wil Books and Documents, 1991), the chapbook *Black Chalk* (Norman: Texture Press, 1992), and in *New and Selected Poems 1961-1996* (San Diego: Junction Press 1997).

CONTENTS

INTRODUCTION

In 1919 Marcel Duchamp bought on the Rue de Rivoli a cheap postcard reproduction of the *Mona Lisa* and decided to give Leonardo's famous enigmatic face a black-penciled mustache, curling up at the corners, and a neat small goatee. Underneath the portrait Duchamp inscribed the letters LHOOQ, a sequence which, read aloud in French, equals *elle a chaud au cul* (she has a hot ass). But his was not just a crude joke; as he explained it many years later, "The curious thing about that mustache and goatee is that when you look at the *Mona Lisa* it becomes a man. It is not a woman disguised as a man; it is a real man, and that was my discovery, without realizing it at the time."

Here Duchamp implies playfully what Freud, in his famous study of Leonardo da Vinci, took very seriously—namely the artist's latent homosexuality. In both cases the model herself (a local merchant's wife) is seen as mere object—"the occasion for these ruses," to use Frank O'Hara's phrase in "In Memory of My Feelings." And of course art historians have taken this object status as given: Ernst Gombrich, for example, argues that the universal appeal of the *Mona Lisa*'s enigmatic smile may be attributed to "Leonardo's famous invention which the Italians call *sfumato*—the blurred outline and mellow colors that allow one form to merge with another and always leave something to the imagination."

Indeed, the painting's *sfumato* does leave something to the imagination, and in her brilliantly inventive *Luca: Discourse on Life and Death* Rochelle Owens has imaginatively recreated Mona Lisa from multiple perspectives, including Mona Lisa's own.

Owens' is a profound meditation on how Leonardo's painting—the very epitome of Renaissance art—was really produced and disseminated, and what the process meant to the women (Mona and her friend Flora, who appears in so many of Leonardo's works) as well as the children who served as models for Jesus and St. John the Baptist in various paintings. Owens' "narrative"—which is complexly disjunctive, weaving in and out of Renaissance Florence, our own time, and the more distant past of pre-Columbian cultures—circles around three characters: "Lenny" (Leonardo) the artist/scientist, the artist's model Mona Lisa, referred to here as Mona or "La Gioconda" ("the smiling woman"), as the painting is also called, and Siggy or Sigmund Freud, whose rationalist analysis destroys the heart and soul of the culture it "murders to dissect." In the course of the narrative Mona and Flora become part of a larger company of women, especially poor women from various Indian tribes, who continue to be oppressed in the Americas of the present:

Leo na r do had not heard you you answer
correctly you calculate the edge reflect

Reflect on the sketch

of Indian women

The conjunction of time frames and situations makes for a bra-
vura performance—that rare long poetic sequence that holds the reader's
attention from beginning to end even though it is by no means a linear
narrative.

Just as Marx will never seem the same after one reads Owens'
Karl Marx Play (1973), so "Lenny" emerges as a complex character, obsessed
with anatomy and hence the dissection of cadavers, much taken with
young boys, alternately giggly and abstracted—and always consumed by
his work. Sigmund is his alter ego—hard, cold, "triumphantly smil[ing]
on reading / a pathological review of a great man." In "The First Person,"
for example, we read:

you said
the smile of Gioconda floats upon

her features   you hook your neck
pursing your lips saturate your dry
eyelids with oil and very lightly

brush in this preherstory widening
your fibrous memory

This passage gives us a good idea of the diction and tone that
distinguish *Luca* from most poetry written today. Owens' theme, here as in
The Joe Poems or *Futz*, is that of violation—the violation of one person's space
by those who want to control or absorb it, who will not let it be. Freud's
"fibrous memory" won't let the Leonardo story be; he has to explain
childhood memories as homosexual fantasies and find explanatory mecha-
nisms for the artist's sublimation. But Owens doesn't relate these things
dispassionately: in her macabre vision Freud is seen "hook[ing] [his] neck"
and, in a horrific image, "saturating [his] dry/ eyelids with oil."

Owens does not shrink from the violence and horror she finds
everywhere around her and which she projects back, most convincingly,
into what was supposed to be, according to Burckhardt and Berenson, the
ordered and measured world of Renaissance Florence. This poet enters her
narrative and calls the shots as she sees them:

At times it seemed
to her she looked like other women

wearing a baffled look her brain
retained an image the very long
teeth due to gum deterioration her

exhaling suddenly looking in the
middle instead holding her head to the
side.

The sardonic suggestion that Mona Lisa's fabled smile is the result of gum deterioration is characteristic of Owens' x-ray vision. Her packed, heavily accented free verse erupts like a volcano, as in this description, early in the poem, of Mona's illness:

Thin body of fiber

Desperately sick for want
of a cleaner wound the woman followed
Mona's orders as if there is any
doubt water   salt   sugar   protein

potassium   calcium   urinate   spon-

taneously then the exposed & opened
entire lens would rupture the rule
in most cases the patient adjusts
following this three to

seven fine sutures of silk or dog-gut.

Notice the strange collision of highly concrete nouns as in lines 5-6 above, with the indeterminacy of reference produced by syntactic ellipsis and a quirky absence of punctuation. In lines 8-9 one expects a period after "rupture," and the next phrase should read, "the rule / in most cases [is that] the patient adjusts, / following this three to seven fine sutures of silk or dog-gut." And even the adjectival modifier here is non-sensical. A surgeon might say, "Give him three to seven sutures" or "He will need three to seven sutures," but in what situation would one say, "following this three to seven fine sutures?" If one knew that Y followed X one would not be in the uncertainty about X that is registered here.

And sound repetition tells the same story. The predominant sound is that of syllables ending with an emphatic /t/ stop: *want*, *salt*, *protein*, *urinate*/ *potassium*, *rupture*, *patient*, *sutures*, *dog-gut*. The poet's voice fairly chokes as it vividly recounts the many threads of the Mona/Flora story—threads that come together later in the poem when the Renaissance motifs are seen through an Aztec prism—words like "Aztec" and "Tlaloc" reinforcing the sound structure of the earlier passages and ironizing the claims of the *conquistadores*, whose plunder of American soil parallels Lenny's earlier plunder of the very bodies and souls of his female models in the interest of anatomical study as well as the art of painting.

Rochelle Owens' writing, here as elsewhere, is *sui generis*. She is, in many ways, a proto-language poet, her marked ellipses, syntactic oddities, and dense and clashing verbal surfaces recalling the long poems of Bruce Andrews and Ron Silliman. But Owens is angrier, more energetic, and more assertive than most of her Language counterparts, male and female, and she presents herself as curiously non-introspective. Hers is a universe of stark gesture, lightning flash, and uncompromising judgement: it is imperative, in her poetic world, to face up to the horror, even as the point of view is flexible enough to avoid all dogmatism.

Immensely learned, sophisticated, and witty in its conceits, this *Discourse on Life and Death* demands two kinds of reading. First, it should be read through from beginning to end as if it were a novel; in this instance, our concern is with character and the interchange between people, and we watch carefully as Mona and Flora and the children evolve before our eyes.

But a second reading is required to note the poem's microstructure—its superb modulation of rhythms and internal rhymes, its ironies and paradoxes. It is the layering of cultures and especially of myths, including our own contemporary myths of the Great Creative Genius (always male), creating beauty out of the detritus around him, that makes *Luca* so distinctive. Watch out, Owens seems to be saying, for those high-minded claims and take another look at the evidence of actual life—"a stream of molten lava burning," "doses of nitrogen muscle saliva," or even "the seams/ of a discarded wallet."

Owens has no easy answers for the pain and sorrow she presents for our contemplation, but her insistent questioning is itself a gift.

Marjorie Perloff

FOR GEORGE:

How shall we sing the Lord's song in a strange land?

The boundaries, limits, and landmarks of the lands,
whose they were
and to whom they belonged.

The countless images refracted from the countless waves of the sea by solar rays where they strike them produce an immense and continuous splendor over the surface of the sea.

Leonardo da Vinci

THE PERSONS

Flora, *a model*
Mona, *another model*
Leonardo, *the artist*
Salia, *Leonardo's student*
Luca, *Leonardo's teacher*

WHITE CLOTH

then in Da Vinci's atelier her
bodice bunched up a mental wagging
signal   she saw snow falling   random
objects such as buttons   pins   felt
wads of string my patch of scalp
tightening 'neath my shimmery hayre

instead of counting
sheep white glass eyes spiritual
flickerings   don't expose your
teeth when you smile   Covered with
a white cloth looking at dried
blood configurations I should not
jump the gun

Reverberating in my heart & stomach
I say my name

The opposite of reflections the solemn
legs under the coarse brown felt
the vomit of the boy configurations
repeating prayers in Latin his cute
packed lederhosen heating up Da Vinci
Flora liked to bring the brat to
torment her tormentor   but instead
Da Vinci is tender like a wet nurse
artful & coy with the tot he has
heard simply the songs of dismember-
ment rasping sound of Lenny breathing

Covered with a white throw looking
at a dead woman lying in the street
A hefty toddler runs up to the cadaver
searching for her shoes   I startle
myself watching Mona's eyes smile
even as the big eyes of the artist
flirt with the boy   The child breaks
into joy shimmering blisters on
his lips

Maneuvering by switching briefly
in essence the corpse has responded
the 10th minute when the experimenter

now stops the slow steady rate in the
center of voluptuousness but then

the boy's abdomen tensed pressing
by hedonism writ large I described
Why in the 13th century this context
combined pleasure & punishment show
that the rhythm a compulsive cycle
Mona didn't imagine for a minute 9
minutes of peace

to press the lever of Da Vinci's notion
to glue the 30 seconds a slow steady logic
after it has pivoted profoundly my head
Mona said needs the stimulus of the laying
on of hands the diversion a sliding hernia
upside-down point of departure

the blocked breath a sense of isolation
the beauty is screwed together

At times it seemed
to her she looked like other women
wearing a baffled look her brain
retained an image the very long
teeth due to gum deterioration her
exhaling suddenly looking in the
middle instead holding her head to the
side   Flora said that she was looking
for her shoes posed like a young
paysanne with smiling little
eyes blushing nostrils   the desperate
pissing need the salty purifying
splash instantly freeing her tightened
eyelids that Da Vinci loved to compare
with a fetus' milky glare   I turn this
funny moment of smirking & place
the whole meaning in a more
fundamental way

mainly shoppers and office workers
watchers a young girl artful smiles
scratching her ankle her peasant dress
reflecting in the window glass oblivious
to the noise of the traffic the moving van
the seven Santini brothers   if I'm holding
my breath before I turn this sentence
around in my head lonely Mona alone
tightening 'neath my shimmery hayre
repeating her name rotating my head to
relax the muscles   She is about to say
something about oil & bread Flora had
fed the boy some while Da Vinci watched
imitating a spider on a mirror circling
the model and the child squaring his
shoulders and screaming in her ears
to roll her tunic up into a ball

Thin body of fiber

desperately sick for want
of a cleaner wound the woman followed
Mona's orders as if there is any
doubt   water   salt   sugar   protein

potassium   calcium   urinate spon-

taneously then the exposed & opened
entire lens would rupture the rule
in most cases the patient adjusts
following this three to

seven fine sutures of silk or dog-gut
Also   it is thought that 2 versions

entire leaves virgin of the cataract
seen once in every thousand births
the polyps manipulated by screaming &

the breaking verses of melancholy like a
panther cub in the middle ear a rim of
keloid tissue transposes Mona

into surgeon after the expulsion

during painful days of sitting
smirking I've inherited a capacity
of childlike rocking & place the
whole meaning in a more fundamental
way

first there is a woman the head of
a hamster in the cup of her hand
eyes mocking & squinting

Mona Posing

of the ovum of a hamster my design
creating the arc in a more fundamental
way my neck contorts in a double-jointed
circle I'm a hungry bum searching
the seams of a discarded wallet

Your patch of scalp shimmering
subtle color through your light brown
hayre

rolling her throat the whistling artful
Mona calmly exhales through the mosquito
netting of the ligament visualized
in transition the speedy walk to the other
end of the street my neck to the side
of the booth hearing the flap of the
leech under the frozen section the
abdominal cavity in a caricature of
a movie-still the whole meaning best begun
before the eyes of Mona Lisa

the fit of the epileptic seeing the wool
of the blanket unravelling agitating
the arc in a more fundamental way
his neck to the side pursing his lips

Da Vinci needed the stimulus of the boy
ripping up the mosquito netting   Mona clamps
the boy's double-jointed knee   the hefty
toddler's tantrum makes Lenny tighten

ligament gray in transition lateral
the design fibrous

hating counting sheep instead
Da Vinci jumps the gun & begins
the story in the middle

pancreatitis inflamation verses of

bile duct fluids & substances exemplify
producing solitary pushing forward the
treachery in medicine completely out of
control it is as if an unusual state of
excitement overtook us & from this even

death may be gist essence

Flora's child had cramps of the hands
that Mona explained as saturation of heat

the skinlike cells of the fresco her
own experiments stimulated by contact
with Machiavelli relaxing sensibly

In this example the influence of the
cunning-eyed Da Vinci visualizing the
first stage a wet blue skin fresh
cadaver the throat muscles still permitting
escape of air Here the old master felt
a longing

SCAR TISSUE

One time he had derided her lower lip
the slanting of her nature she said
Mauve & gray splendid engineering the
passage of throat to jaw so that

the weight of the feverish boy his
knees pushed towards her body angling
superimposing itself oddly on her
shoulders transforming

& defying classifications into dozens

of broken edges child & Da Vinci perched
on Mona's back

peasant dress & slanting smile
bitter earwax taste in the cleft

Slowly you startle while slowly
you depict the icy dots
of the spiritual condition
You arch your foot   your eyes
small & hard & round with disgust

shaping her lips a neat crack in
the center   the natural environment
a wilderness of monkeys   the nose
of Da Vinci dribbled while she
posed   I watch the pattern
of his hand Mona   Flora's brat
writhes & twists about so many
tricks up his sleeve   she was only
here by accident   In the atelier
carefully she put the lukewarm salt
water into the cup of her hand
the sun would not have blazed nor
the trees become green nor Mona
smirking   As if you could be normal
with the dead woman's sewing needle
sticking into a ball of felt
Outside an arc of sticks & stones

mounds of infectious waste in
the middle

the red & black cadavers odor of
silent red clay

your patch of scalp shimmering
subtle color through your light brown
hayre

peasant dress & slanting smile
bitter earwax taste in the cleft

Once he merrily laughed contorting
his neck so that he looked dead for
a split second

Like a bright cartoon the big
teeth & gums

biological destiny the prehistoric
beginnings Mona potato cut he couldn't
avert his cunning eyes   Mona got into
the act   I've got weaving eyes she said
clamping her hand on the cadaver's femur

my brain is popping with pictures
Panavision Panaflex cameras Mona
breathing a continuation thin wispy
hairs circling her knuckles deep purple
eyes severe imbalance of her vermillion
pretty mouth

a ball of felt is my artistic goal melon
polyester she said smoothing the child's
feverish head plopping an egg into a
bowl inserting an ancient spoon judging
by the flourish of the leaves spreading
into dots

Slowly you startle while slowly
you depict the icy dots of the spiritual
condition

You arch your foot your eyes small &
hard & round with disgust

Flora sings the dried mucus pretty as
a star she's watching for a day to leave
the little turd this afternoon I was
going to pose for Da Vinci but Mona
is my friend

Permanent Supply

Hating counting sheep instead
Da Vinci jumps the gun & begins
the story in the middle   but then
the boy's abdomen tensed the breath
blocked between his heart & stomach

Born near Vinci Mona entered a
medieval atmosphere a copy of her
survives buried black in the museum
her distance phobia from the voyeurs
that mouth good evening sonnet
sequences relating her cunningly
made fibonacci facial harmonies
his exquisite brushstroke flourishes
& twirls   undefeated mistrust   &

the child's quickened heart-shaped
heinie swaddled in guiltless lederhosen
the enigmatic roving-eyed boy

the largest becoming the young St.
John the dumb amiable undeveloped
fetal glance expanding Da Vinci's
reputation   alchemists had their
day plugging hanging on entering
the service of the household acting
inhuman at times moaning about two
versions & idylls of love & nature

The Substitute

of the ovum of a hamster my design
creating the arc in a more fundamental
way   so that his cute heinie garbed
in lederhosen so sturdy he is resembles
the curve of a valentine heart

My neck contorts in a double-jointed
circle   I'm a hungry bum searching

the seams of a discarded wallet
But the boy acted so inhuman at
times tugging on the cloth of the
table or his mother's apron strings

I had a gargantuan curiosity
my notebooks input-output a vast
panther of expertise sot Whitman
would have recognized political
& social depths in addition analysis
of sfumato deadly pebbles in the
female breast I became a close friend
of Flora who was a model for Da Vinci
Here I found the field of medicine
dominated by artful imitators tricks
up their sleeves making gut scrotums
instead of splitting open their con-
clusions

invention composition geology botany
the portrait of the enigmatic fetus-eyed
merchant's wife revealing a wish-bone
shaped diagnostic tool I learned from
her devices & skills to study swamp
reclamation projects & spots of the
limbs & place the meaning

Keeping in condition a model's trick
I say in a lyrical tone & you don't know me
He wants to identify with
me

sitting here yesterday scratching my
mosquito bites I then pose like a
muscle-man   eyes frozen   sucking
my cheeks in sanity's bubbling &
gurgling noises as the old stage
magician watches me massage my scalp

transfixed by a drawing of a seizure

I hook my neck even further
& close my teeth over my lips

who heard the murmurs   a stab wound
anatomy its messages stenosis of the
aortic valve clicks scratchy dysfunction
Mona wrote dead on her feet

I was not a little surprised I bend
& listen to the child who scratched
his face   Flora believed she decoded
the most purely   I enter the rolled
up cylinder then in Da Vinci's diseased
brain I find that I could perceive Mona's
authority splashing of her urine her
scanning the air near the end of the
ear the boy propelling blood but for

Lenny poignant was the name of Mona
viewing the paralysis her face took
on a stupid languid mask Da Vinci
questioned first then giggled then
satisfied my surgical curiosity

He was the da vin ci leonar do da
vin ci painter sculptor architect
musician engineer and scientist Mona

perforated his skull leading into
the reversible procedure   cheerfully
he places the stillborn cross-eyed
memory back into place

She was the illegitimate daughter she

32

passed her adolescence winters are long
in Vinci she had an enduring interest
in newspaper photographs and television

dysfunction workload the meaningless
light of new information a click or
clicks may cease with the first child
the mitral valve   In an early source I
described his beauty & charm fundamental
crumbling iconoclast

bleeding the preliminary
the end locked anonymous the whitish
crossing herself defines the wife of
a Florentine merchant

worked Mona and summers
are really cruel said bean-eyed Flora

but then the boy's abdomen tensed
the breath locked

the power of invention lost notebooks
of Mona she had worked on a model of
an equestrian monument served as
consultant in Piombino même
montrant le respect pour le juif Ezra
lofty in feeling as those projects
demanded   Mona solitary nocturnal
became my close friend   her long
gray hands sickly foxheads said
the aging master admiring the anatomical

studies multiple versions of distended
uterus malformations anonymous prostitutes
donating their fetal tissue without a
qualm the breath locked   uselessly
she applied the treatment

her slanting mouth opened

the gate has closed behind them said
the child playing with the keys locks

little chains of Lenny who whenever he was
able would violate ooze out in
intakes of thin sound

between the heart & stomach she
detailed all the interruptions

creating my design   picture plane
at the confluence Leonardo Mona said
agitating the arc in a more fundamental
way   But the cycle of anxious
searching is an addictive code whined Flora

on the examining table every interpretation
writ large so that neither powerlessness
nor the bright yellow phobia   begins
to crumble   the secret burns on the cadaver's

scalp that pulled the hair out frightened
the boy   But Lenny at rest diagnosed a
series of complex chemical dyes thus spent
the tears of the brat the characteristic

growth pattern evaluated by Mona   a child
of six   moon-active smiled Lenny in a
poetic mood   I remember said Lenny when I
was six years old before I knew Mona or
Flora   at dusk & at night I was visited
by a leopard with long whitish fur

at the same time my tutor who liked to
box & who had a quizzical look much like
Mona had before I changed it to cunning-
eyed for the portrait at least opposite

Your patch of scalp shimmering
subtle color through your light brown
hayre

I said a work is a mutation & does not
breed true but it's a distinct species
patterned like the portrait of the wife

of a Florentine merchant   The hefty
toddler runs up to my feet solidly sits
down backwards his heart-shaped heinie
swaddled in guiltless lederhosen

sounds   the lup-pud   that scratched near
the mosaic decoration   condemned crunch

after a stab wound a small pinch into
the chest   interpreted wrongly   the arcane
antifreeze   there is much to learn Mona
whistled   to the boy to be helpful but
too independent as usual he squatted
down his heart-shaped heinie swaddled in

guiltless lederhosen binding in the presence
of the old master   making Lenny stare the
atelier becoming like a civil holiday
infected with play as bright as a yellowish
red tropical fruit   but Flora put the
manacles on to stop the degree of suspicion

a cord dangling from the ceiling to the
floor engrossed the boy twisting about
spilling fruit juice time-consuming scintill-
ation I was visited   into limbo those projects
demanded closed distance Flora was looking
as usual for her shoes that the nervy brat
had shoved behind the loose tile   my love

gallops sang Leonardo mastering his unconscious
benignly   more than this can be harmful awkward
somewhat the unsmiling paysanne

with cunning eyes rolled her moon-gray
shoulders nodded yes   lay your probe
down essential outlines obstruction a vivi-
fying principle exalted paling shimmering
deafening quadrupled view   attentive   only

my neck hooked forward gifted higher &
wider drifting the glance of Mona centrifugal

the invader across my mind   the crevice
the grout is in   a little space

get the details right   the introverted
part captured grasped   if you knew the

sounds the lup-pud that scratched near
the mosaic decoration

she gets obsessed by it maneuvering by
switching her interpretation

but then the boy's abdomen tensed
the breath locked

So you had this experience & it burned
you up   she had what she calls an experience
relentless ton of bricks   I became offended
she wasn't going to the atelier often
enough   she knew the situation

you arch your foot your eyes small &
hard & round with disgust

the one hand   the conviction a couple
of monks snooping   sneaking into the atelier
something is going on inside Lenny's
space   very suspicious shadowy things
eating up folklore   look her slanting
mouth a cup of gold light wriggling
without a qualm   I'm a hungry bum
searching the seams of a discarded
wallet grudging habits a bunch of
wives rounded up

collections   the detached gray cortex
sexist

using flattened fingers attentive only
to the massage the thought reflects the
paysanne smirking

LENNY SAYING

the patient warm in the film scenario
A nest of grasses

reflects the paysanne   the toe of her
shoe first sound defined when the tap
is knocked loose   you startle yourself
watching my peasant dress reflecting
in the window glass   my solemn legs
under the coarse folds   outside the brain
of the dead woman is studied
the child watches digging with a stick
in the mud

I am aware of Flora placing her ear
on the patient's chest

you arch your foot your eyes small &
hard & round with disgust

flat soft eyes   probing the mud
the child runs up to the cadaver searching
for her shoes   even as the big eyes
of the artist flirt with the boy

I said a work is a mutation & does not
breed true but it's a distinct species

flat soft sounds   the little leather
sandals of the child   he's looking at
a horizontal timber sneaks past Lenny
finds one of the storerooms open

fragments of broken oil & wine storage
jars

I am the sterile man said Leonardo
whose enigmatic smile came out of a
skin suture   I imitated simply without
any conscious decision   giggled Flora
before dressing   into the veins the
third utilization of painful process

making the type of procedure done coldly
without tension slides fixed & stained
my curiosity fails to explain the question
behind the external flows the midline
has been marked   It comes to women I
went to a conference last year   a woman
on the loose   I could learn Latin I said
I am committed to the humanities   I am
the last inheritor Mona said sincerely

Spanish princess and southern nuns
the jewel of mathematics jesus christ
contradicted the rigors of the network
docudrama chanted Lenny   Mathematics is
a delicious ocean   it does all the work
smiling Mona said   Somehow the boy grabbed
the diagnostic tool   the aging master in
a frenzy shook the lederhosened brat of
Flora saturated his limbs with a cold
solution   but then embraced him like
the Virgin I was not a little surprised
judging by the crumbling 10th minute of
waiting endlessly for the results

unknown going on in the body of the dead
woman   lazily Mona touches the tightened
eyelids that Lenny loved to compare
with a fetus' milky glare   translated
the fibers

felt small sections   were corrupt just
north of the extremity   within the boy's
sharpness   in the atelier exactly 4 o'clock
the hefty toddler runs up to the cadaver

I saw Lenny   in the light   he had torn
a fragment quietly muttering   is this that
which moved   accented deep words   guarding
the lovely portrait deepening the folds
of the dress   the paysanne having no definite
quiver in her depths   faint echoes   in a
vast prolonging the same pristine expanse
dissolving

The large barrier evaporated   the handwriting
of Mona bathed the sinuous curve the moving
without parcelling of authorship   two letters
or three & again you have no way of combining
the filled open distance limited only by Mona's
existence   posed   outside the infectious waste
the reddish hair of Lenny every crime of
falsified contributions to science recorded

noted analyzed listened to the sounds of the
body   my body oriented towards the atelier
where the young wife of the Florentine merchant
structures the small stones about her   corner
in the atelier   the pile of debris   was higher
than the geometric design that bordered the
oily mosaic of the wall   the floral design
into dozens of broken edges

child & Da Vinci perched on the donkey's back
a tile hiding the cupboard where the artist
hid his narcotics   making up the stories
not wanting to be identified with the assoc-
iationists   no existence of moment

objective   the placement the depths
of me   every event the present that
appears the things

dissembled   she sees the region explod-
ing   and Mona herself   all her skin
converged creating multiple boils

plague discovers space plague of a
world   her will radiates extended
without a fixed the punctual dispersion

a dog's barking rolling his eyes
fear of catching the disease   in whirls
of projections

covered with a white throw looking
at a dead woman lying in the street
the stones about her but instead Flora

patiently waits traversing the animal
kingdom I am destitute of obsession
you arch your foot your eyes small &

hard & round with disgust plague under-
neath the coarse brown felt the vomit of
the boy   but Mona studied broken images

keeping a cunning eye from object to
object without budging sinuous conscious-
ness   little by little plague covers

space   breaks away spontaneous plague
new & clean enlarging its incessant
swelling   in Mona's posing

the thought that the model
is looking out

the maximum of distance   pleasing
to Mona   water compresses the easel

but then the doors of the atelier
I imagine you revolving   only Mona is
the place 50 percent of her
moving grace traced   a simple anarchy
fixed to the circumference   the wheel
of Lenny's digging down

but then I make the hours at once
she said systematic defining my interval

of rage the blood vessels of the skin
my nervous system ranging from flying
machines to caricatures seductive

energy   A hefty toddler his cute
packed lederhosen heating up Da Vinci
Flora liked to bring the brat to
torment her tormentor   the curve of
a valentine heart as he solidly
squats & tortures   strange sweet odor
exhales in proportion to the intact

murmurs of the aging master alone
in a diseased valve of strange
kinds of repetitive work   integrated
control of fright

begins to crumble   an arc of sticks
& stones   a fiberoptic light source
distended unexpected leaf pattern of
shimmering mucus in the middle
you're watching him massage

begins at 7:45 a.m. philosophy the
women Flora said

running the household   I suppose to
help one another jealousy & quarreling
what to do & what not to do

a bunch of men in an isolation

tower   lonely with cunning eyes they
are suffering from liver abscess due
to stones & strictures   undercutting
the women   Flora said Mona smiled
too much excommunicated splinter

sect of benign unexamined life not
worth living a bit of rough edges
my kidney rests near my soul mocked
Mona   my quadruple choice decompresses
centering at the living spontaneous
with extreme molecular slowness

be an eye to see it   that I could
perceive   the caricature of the Mona
Lisa with a cigar in her mouth
The degree of suspicion tightening
Lenny's eyelids damning Flora for
not having been the model   his first
choice & the child squaring his
shoulders & screaming in her eyes

eyes of Mona Lisa in transition
awakened exclusive focus backward
the boy breaks into joy while
Lenny watches pursing his lips
learning you're a hungry bum searching
the seams of a discarded wallet

There is one thing
that obtrudes itself   this Renaissance
case of dementia præcox

at the time my tutor who liked to box

Your patch of scalp shimmering
subtle color through your light brown
hayre

I had this appetite which was implanted
said Lenny when I was six years old
sighing nocturnal pollutions hysteria
oft times I am like a woman
increased reflex excitability
of my female generative organs

With cunning eyes rolled her moon-gray
shoulders nodded yes
the invader across my mind

inscrutable the memory vulture conceals
nothing at the same time a thought obtrudes
smiled Lenny in a poetic mood

impulse and his atelier is full of
stone splinters   and   dust now his
face is smeared and powdered

she gently and very lightly brushes
in the beautiful colors the lup-pud
of the paint the turning configurations
black art

fragments from Mona's life & age
grouped around laughing feminine heads

the incubus stories fascinated her
she arranged them in two or more sets
interposing the internal Egyptian structure
theory with her own   that is to break in

on the interruption itself with a conscious
twist in parallel lines arguing with Flora
whether one ought   to meditate or pray first
Flora said no just do it coldly

you arch your foot your eyes small
& hard & round with disgust

I re-evaluated the misery that a
patient will take a stimulus diluted
& adulterated enough to chain

the boy down & nail him to a rock
catching his shrieks in cups of gold

But the cycle of anxious searching
said Leonardo like a chinese fairytale
Flora lied   risk & compulsion you said

I startle myself watching Mona's eyes
smile even as the big eyes of the artist
flirt with the boy

but the cycle itself a deranged pattern
entails a midline in which the backward
rather than the forward shock obstructs
the heart wall I wondered touching the
facial nerve   the appearance of the face
looks a little crazy like a master boxer
probably an Athenian or a Tuscan Da Vinci
giggled   underneath the two big brothers

is the evening sky in April

Artfully Making Up

Lenny only once interspersed in his
scientific descriptions a communication
from his childhood

I should not jump the gun
only definite information
the flight of the vulture

the breaking verses of melancholy

I entered as apprentice   it is not
known in what year   in the studio

of Andrea del Verrocchio.

In 1472 Leonardo's name could already
be found in the register of the members
of the "Compagnia dei Pittori"

That is all

that I should occupy myself
so thoroughly with the vulture

for it comes to my mind

light wriggling without a qualm
I'm a hungry bum searching the seams
of a discarded wallet
I suddenly interrupt myself in order
to follow up a memory

her eyes pressed said Flora seeing
me snake-dance across the floor
Mona breathing a continuation
a young girl artful smiles
posed like a young paysanne

simple taken   relation   form
point   movement   but   dynamism in

planisphere frozen   prism   fluid
but then the boy's abdomen tensed
the breath blocked

red manacles   cord dangling to
bring to the ambitious state of a
state of suspicion opening & shut
case   fraud posed a young girl
artfully making up her eyes looks

around   a dead ringer she fears
for her life expanding rasping to
perfection your glance deducts in
pain infected with play digging a
hole flat soft sounds neutral bug
crawling under the cuffs of Flora

Mona believed melancholy
mentally looking at the lever
rigidity exalted invading my head
even as the solemn legs under the

coarse folds the laying on of oil
pigment rotating the brush breath
pivoting on the skinlike cells of
the portrait I turn this funny
essential zone

now a hole in expanding
the invading grout is in a small
space broken storage mosaics

constantly she said what effects
the glimpse texture glass fiber what
effects the intense secrecy

the intrigue in the atelier while
Mona practiced dismembering

Flora whispered   several years ago
redesigned the conclusion indicated
by its shape   I have no   doubt

fluctuating between the sharp edge
within a small radius the external flows
exposing hazardous materials what

grim effects the intense composite
outbreak of illnesses rashes nausea
memory lapses blood in the stool

a suction device stuck in the grout
state of suspicion Mona held the tool
cleansing of the degenerative

matter causing premature senility
confided Flora I worked for two days
on this one-eighth-inch-thick white

composite material while Leonardo watched
pursing his lips at the misdeeds of
the brat three stolen golden chains
this pre-history of benign unexamined
be an eye to see it and dust now
my face is smeared and powdered
artfully made up

THE MODEL RELAXES

all over the painted plaster the dumped
rubble which had been flung higgledy-
piggledy

to excavate   the pace of the work there
were pillars the huge pile of earth the
greatest bargain on down

mosaics these mosaic floors double walls
sealing the moisture in   as soon as the
model relaxes   lapse of time Flora is my
good friend she let me pose today because
the blood acts as an aphrodisiac swarming
intertwining   the space of excavation

from the south porch of the atelier at
least ten minutes the brat played sitting
down tossing several stones white mosaic
stones V-shaped patterns forming geometric
hexagons in black stone the ceiling in the
atelier broken edges dozens of nervous
lyrical slowness   to touch the facial nerve
Mona endures her absence   finally the

floating ligament between the space detached
from the glance

expressing her own interior unvaryingness
deafening the model while the boy chewed
up hazel-nuts spitting them out in her hand
Lenny smelling the tot's vigorous curve
of knee and calf the artist breaks into

coughs the painted plaster flaking broken
oil and vin

and contemptuous in feeling dead flesh
her notebooks filled with white noise
but the thumb of the boy scratching a cacophony
of sound

rose like a column of blood 'neath your
shimmery hayre

& the subsequent first sound works   the murmur
of the instrument bores through

the outer cage inhaled   becomes this fear
idiocy reveals a glimmer of intelligence
learned step by step   impulse innocent hello
whines Da Vinci

Flora said that she transmitted messages
from the lederhosened brat   mold & bacteria
eat the same food   her lips were smiling
sealing the fate of the dead woman temporarily
loosened circulation twenty seconds collections
in the depths of the gray cortex detached
but Mona said that if I look beneath the jaw
bones having all the facts

I'm a hungry bum searching the seams
of a discarded wallet

The flat piece structural characterized in
Lenny's imaginary world floating in urine
of rabbit & squirrel the flow shaking the
fixed rules demolishing & wriggling forward
indiscriminately   Flora said the boy had
caught a chill & was fussing   he couldn't
stop screaming squeezing his eyes shut
shimmering mucus on his lids

pressed against the tip is a
painter   I should not jump the gun
switching the manacles congestive
the strain stone crushing but Flora

said there is much to learn from her
brat   seeing him snake-dance across
the floor

Flora liked to bring to the ambitious
work running down the opulent decor
to show that they had not intentionally

48

set on fire the atelier what evidence
was in the hiding place I'm a hungry
bum searching the seams reverberating

the child runs up to the flaccid cystic
tube construction his mouth imitating
Mona's a state of wonder dropped disappear
abdomen stained so that cellular details
exquisite like stars into compulsive dots
combined pleasure & pain the reddish eyes
of Lenny

aiming for simplicity it was only here
& there running from east to west the
white mosaic stones bearing a simple
geometric pattern of hexagons in black
stone why did she choose a location
disintegrating at the touch of a hand

only a few pieces there was no sign
except a heap of mosquito netting
a curious kind of arrangement observed
Mona

a moving van moving south   seen
from   aerial photo   unevenness of
the ground   sounds of   broken

& burned about six feet high light plastered
walls close to the floor the southwest
the stroke   symbol   cure

Flora & Lenny eating white beans
watching   child snake-dance towards
the hiding place Sleep more   after
the portrait is finished Mona will
sleep more you said   very bottom
of   muscle is odd congested
function of   atelier crossed over

a hill village in Tuscany   region
outstanding   surgeon will often
perform a mock operation to reinforce

the contemplation   awakened exclusive
focus

limitation experience   used image
to devour   vibration of multiplicity

the white throw covers   cadaver
she's watching for a day to leave
the space of mucus shimmering

searching plants & parts extracted
from   whole so named a skin border
becomes obscured   thing   renders Flora
horizon   the disc like a wall hiding
stifled lonely Mona alone
tightening 'neath my shimmery hayre
deepening   the face looks posed
like a young paysanne

MONA POSES INSTEAD

I have decoded this permits
continued growth the muscle inflammation
common for one week

shatterproof & unbreakable I'm
structuring patiently the depths
of the muscle   inflamation constant
exhaling I turn the objects randomly

to me I look like others   I say my
name Da Vinci this afternoon Flora was
going to pose but Mona is her friend
a ball of felt is her artistic goal
melon polyester   she couldn't avert
her cunning eyes

I'm a hungry bum searching the seams
of a discarded wallet even as the big eyes
of the brat flirt

I clamp the boy's double-jointed knee
hating counting sheep instead Da Vinci
jumps the gun

objective repeating prayers in Latin
his cute packed lederhosen the old master
felt a longing

that I eat white beans with Flora & Mona
watching the boy snake-dance towards
the hiding place

hearing the flap of the leather sandals
the external flows

respond now there's rapid visible
light pushing the barbed fitting
in a combined sorting present reflects
purges connects for optimum imaging

then in Da Vinci's atelier looking
at dried blood configurations

exhaling I turn the portrait around
your patch of scalp shimmering
subtle color through your light brown
hayre

state of suspicion breathing Mona
clamps her hand on the cadaver's femur
distrusts her glance the breaking verses
of melancholy her lower lip bitten

interpreted wrongly across my eyes
the gift of the portrait of the Florentine
merchant's wife in essence the experimenter

that she was looking for her shoes
see her tightened eyelids

posed like a young paysanne dominating
at dusk & at night before I knew
Mona hearing the flap of the abdominal
cavity fibrous circles the depths

of the edge of the masterpiece burnt
on the left side

the blocked breath & punishment she
was the illegitimate daughter passed
her adolescence winters are long
in Vinci

Why   at the end of the 20th century
the laying on of hands

the boy's abdomen tensed combined
pleasure & punishment show that upside-
down the lever of Da Vinci's logic

a slow steady rate at the end of your
century Mona turns relaxes her muscles
holding her breath lonely Mona alone
scratching her ankle her peasant dress

colored with the dye of salt sugar protein
patient slow during days of sitting
smirking

I've inherited a capacity of childlike
rocking & place the whole meaning

in most cases the patient adjusts

I watched Da Vinci who is about to say
something about oil & water

with a fetus' milky glare Da Vinci
artful smiles his body angling toward
the burnt left corner visualizing
his body angling transforming & defying
nature she couldn't avert her cunning
eyes Mona

slow molecular smile the sun would not
have blazed nor the trees greened

Flora's brat writhes & twists

she was only here by accident in the
atelier carefully she put the lukewarm
salt water into the cup of her hand

mitral the alarm from the equal end
mitral bore & length mitral filter
knocking rubbing the light sounds that
revealed new sources after the fire
we found a few filters a light mitral
valve situated

it could be one of the tasks said Mona
in a second shifting her hip revolting
against her position she felt like
having a warm bath slightly she pressed
the corner of her eyelid down closer
examination of the portrait disturbing

the chagrin the paint was still fresh
she continued thinking about glue into

the plaster that the child had discovered
felt like playing with on the edge of the
terrace

rains burst the pipes & the work stopped
it was Mona's desire to rest to study
to focus the spot expanding her own middle

you arch your foot you have heard simple
keloid tissue alarm the numbered sheep
her labored posing melancholy enigmatic
inhuman

so that his cute heinie garbed in
lederhosen so sturdy he is resembles
the curve of a valentine heart

contorts her neck undefeated mistrust
& the child's quickened heart-shaped
song

coldly numbering the codifications
clamping my hand on the nervy brat

always touching things
the shroud   14 feet   3 inches long
3 feet   7 inches wide bears faint

slowly I paid a heavy debt

bears faint hidden forms

bears the faint blood-stained image
of a whipped and crucified woman

Mona intoned but Flora dismissed it
as forgery

your transferred fixated
the white burial cloth mesmerizes

numbered named I should not jump
the gun maneuvering

Mona says theorizing what might be
grouped combined accumulated coded
collected the substances

onto the shroud   14 feet   3 inches long

death may be gist essence

the sketch fueling you

the atelier filled with busts statues
funerary altars grouped

grim exposed it bears faint
bears faint hidden forms
searching the remains of cremations

Flora intoned without end
14 feet   3 inches long   the shroud

bears faint hidden forms
the patient adjusts during painful
days of lying

bears the faint blood-stained image
of a whipped and crucified woman

I should not jump the gun maneuvering
coldly I preserve details numbering
the codifications   Mona intoned but
Flora dismissed it as forgery

it ought to be Lenny hung on a cross
underpaying the apprentices

slowly   I   paid a heavy debt

maneuvering the text
onto the shroud   one can sit wondering

in the same position thinks Mona

nailed into space

I would like to restrain

so that his cute heinie garbed in
lederhosen so sturdy he is resembles
the curve of a valentine heart

slowly I mesmerize

reconstruct facts of the inscrutable
portrait tighten the shroud

slowly I paid a heavy debt

3 feet   7 inches wide   bears faint
hidden forms bears the faint blood-stained

image of a whipped and crucified woman
Mona intoned   but Flora dismissed
it as forgery

the middle of her story blood-stained

nailed into space

while others dismiss me slowly
I mesmerize

dismiss me as a clever craftswoman
you search for the cremains

riddle of the shroud into the fibers
mistrusts her notebooks rewritten
Mona's brain averts

prototypes of paintings ransacked
image fueling Flora posing

her hip revolting against her position
she felt like having a warm bath

as you search accumulated forms

the work stopped & rains burst
the pipes

I am only here by accident

disenchanted my words photograph
the shroud when with chain saw saw
the faint blood-stained image

the degree of maneuvers of the chain
saw the configurations saw snow falling
random devastation battlegrounds

and wearing my peasant dress saw the
chain in the middle composite of the
dead woman lying in the street
related compositional prototypes
four corners of the world

blood and strewn with hand-written
words on the masterpiece saw the
ransacked atelier after the fire

wrath deciphered by flames   riddle
of the white throw   14 feet   3 inches
long 3 feet   7 inches wide   bears faint
hidden forms   bears the faint blood-stained
circles   mistrusts your notebooks
describing the methods exposed the
fetus' milky glare to that unfathomable
smile   you are only here

in the space of Mona's atelier
sitting down & forcing burning views
coldly I preserve details while

numbering   a sense of isolation death
may be gist essence   see me going from
the center   separates contracts   see
Mona going

Frightened of Exposure

while slowly the pattern of
logic objects smashing   shoved back
the scientific texts on

the face of it

while slowly the pattern of
her hand delicately touching a rim
of the glass

the interior prized it reminds Mona
of two portraits propped backwards
a neat crack in the center two volumes

deliberately worked

devour bits visualized in transition
unrelated to objects smashing
converging numbering the scientific
works of Mona substantial grouped
deliberately

her resistance of imitation consists
embodied buried black in the museum
trusts her glance theorizing the image
was caused

a belief implanted when she was

scrutinizing the precise texts on
the face of it the portrait is a steady

logic drawing attention until scientific
studies accumulate a photographic
negative

telling of the other things
she saw there   she looked up and saw
hand-written words on the masterpiece
saw the atelier after the fire saw
whirling wrath in the space

with the middle feet Lenny clasped
his belly sang the brat softly

saw the ransacked atelier after the
fire

I saw two portraits propped against
each other   the air full of the remains
of cremations   mistrusts her notebooks
the facts exposed through a prism
diagnosed numbered

then Lenny biting himself in great joy
laughed the child

your patch of scalp shimmering
subtle color through your light brown
hayre

riddle of the burial cloth the boy
sucking   thievish   mendacious   willful
gluttonous

Lenny accused frightened of exposure

Flora's eyes round with disgust

Concerning Lenny we have to take the
view that he was only here by accident
of his illegitimate birth

concerning Mona who claimed devotion
years after the shroud appeared

devotion woven into the coarse brown
felt the vomit simply as belief or
disgust

moved the passionate pilgrim consumed
the news screwed mistrust condemned
the fraud the type of procedure done

coldly meant to distance herself she
had torn a fragment peeled a layer

seeing the cunning maneuvers that
interspersed this prebreath

I wanted to bring the twofold image
one woman portrayed related deemed

the sun would not have blazed nor
the trees become green nor Mona smirking

your slanting mouth opened   I said a
work is a mutation

I'm a hungry bum searching the seams
of a discarded wallet

volcanic ash dust and triggered fires
limited only by Mona's breathing
the solemn legs under the coarse brown
felt the configurations a wilderness

cellular details slow molecular

cunningly highlighted the gaps in
the middle of my story

my work into Mona's work beachcombing
aspects triggered fierce

passing into episodes mass extinctions
you are about to see stuck in the grout
unearthed without end backwards

events in the atelier exposed ridiculed

the black art

snow falling I focused isolated
into the fibers' capricious authority
I began my work Flora said opening
wrath in the space embedding numbering

circles despised the degree   watching
my eyes in a time the nervy brat

had shoved grout filled up anatomical

stricken with love it reminds Mona
then seeks how the shroud was made
shoved back faint blood-stained

Mona who loved theorized

that you could see faint despised
misdiagnosed loose particles burning
snow

fabricated by a pseudoartistic
sleight of hand diligently manipulating
with the passion of avarice

that the shroud had been fashioned
and how the said cloth breathed in
my heart & stomach   looking at the
the solemn legs under the coarse

felt searching the layers wearing
a baffled look   I watched purified
versions jump the gun

I remember said Mona a certain cloth
cunningly painted symptoms scanning

that the shroud had been fashioned
Flora decided with a theatrical authority
cunning growth

complex chemical dyes subtle color
through your light brown hayre

and how the cloth said breath in
the image sonnet sequences patterned
like the portrait of the merchant's
wife

at the same time my tutor with a
sleight of hand space broke invading

my state of suspicion this is an ambitious
work of genius   my slow molecular smile

structuring aptly patiently blood in
the stool transformed the plaster dumped
rubble constantly she said I worked for
two days on this one-eighth-inch-thick
white composite conclusion redesigned

the flow shaking forward

rose like a column of blood 'neath your
shimmery hair

subject matter   expands day
beginning in the middle clenched
pressed together   for almost 1,000
years traumatized

I should not jump the gun awakened
in me reflection   suddenly the selections
described by Mona

puckered the left corner of her mouth

Flora & Mona reading Lenny's notations
silver brocade   trimmed velvet a
lira here a lira there
a fresh melon for the brat

mistrusts his accounts the snake-dance
of the ledger cost of oil and wax
erotic Christian art far ahead of
her time

because it is not the intent of experts to mislead

in whose being one seems to expose
the facts   searching the enigmatic smile

I have only painted compulsively
diagnosed numbered sometimes laughing
crooning to the brat

a curious kind of derangement
seven days sitting delineation of god

behind the opaque sketch the molecular
wrath expertise deepening the explanation

smacking into the theory for
rival theories   I saw thin layers
arrangements impacted global climate

one point accidental always fueled
Nemesis Mona scrutinizes slowly
measures numbers coldly artful

holding her head to the side

and wearing my peasant dress gathered
puckered linen fires sunlight changes
trusts herself isolated

in the service of the number of
stone splinters grouped accumulated
full of stone splinters and dust

efforts of the hammer pounding widening
the fragment traced to a unique
point silent isolated

undisturbed concerning Lenny who
loved beauty that he always trembled
at the sight

I focused and photographed his wasting
time   his slack deceptions tricky sleight
of hand accounts falsified

my contradictions in dry words I
blamed his secrecy his hunger willful
sucking circular

subject matter   scientific cold

then seeks how the shroud was
made riddle accused

we have to take the views into
Mona's brain my century in the end

ransacked faint blood-stained
hidden forms crosses circles

arrangements of structure   only
one single accidental point
the transparent sketch

the raw data normal and nervous
image of a whipped and crucified
woman
the key to the code covered with
a white throw   looking at a dead woman
covered with a white cloth

into the fibers of the shroud
breathing all significance

the ransacked atelier after the fire
she is only here scrutinizing
searching

when she dissected cadavers of horses
and human beings
I am covered with small marble splinters
see me going from the center
numbering in those things absorbed
deviated

the intersection cutting   real space
necessity saint's halo the black line
fails

shifts towards accumulated grouped
subject matter   stripes of spirituality
that Mona once falsified when she

dissected cadavers vibrant abstract
reverberations blood-stained white over
black   the shroud chromatic   the twofold
image a seam texturing wanting to
violently curve the drawing

limited the hammer pounding Flora's
face looks gently back towards the wall

splinters and dust slow molecular the sun
unchained   whips doubt

then Lenny biting himself smacking
the altar   Mona focused diagnosed theorized
shows the shroud   that unfathomable
growing dead blood bears

the riddle shredded fashioned with
falsity regret when she was trusting
the forger

and wearing my peasant dress breathing
a continuation smoothing my feverish head
drawing the merchant's wife posing

her cunningly made fibonacci facial
deformations

alchemists inhuman data

I'm a hungry bum searching the seams
of a discarded wallet

The First Person

Mona's text began   as if an unusual
state of excitement overtook me

I focused   my body angling superimposing
I saw thin layers treachery in medicine
widening control it is as if

the passage of throat to jaw nor Flora
smirking   as if you could be spiritual
in the atelier

slowly you startle while slowly
you depict the icy dots   Flora sings
about two versions

so that his cute heinie garbed
in lederhosen so sturdy he is resembles
the curve of a valentine heart

keeping in condition an artist's trick
you say in a lyrical tone & I don't
know you   I long to identify I have a
drawing valid mustachioed Mona

to write leaving in its wake reverberations
Lenny who loved to theorize

smeared and powdered with marble dust
luster fashioned with honesty spotlessly
hardly anything is known guided by his
trembling impulse

the pale gray image ruled a current
slow absorption riveted depth exerting
steadiness unchained moved the edge

texturing the configurations trimmed
velvet a lira here a lira there very
early in the morning and did not leave

spaces between two bony areas
sect between benign unexamined tasks
I whispered ill of the dead

inserting fatal caricatures of
Lenny said Sigmund whetting our
palates said Flora millions

of manipulations a pathological
review of a great man searching
the seams of a discarded wallet

changing a light bulb the merchant's
wife thought of Sigmund's words
"the inhibitions in Lenny's

sex life and his artistic activity."

backward focus the point where Mona
Flora Lenny the child jostle for
the attention jealousy & quarreling

of what to do & what not to do

the tutor of Lenny a piece of senseless
impertinence to make a study of things
in him that could just as easily
be found

in the first person one came across

Mona triumphantly smiled on reading
this breathing you have heard simply
the sound of my insatiable design

her first choice the woman covered
with a white throw

Why   in the end of the century this
context the fabled diversion

I described expanded my second choice
you reasoned tightening a light

she sealed the hiding place that
they maneuvered that the cycle
we isolated the rhythm to the left of
us grouping the breaking verses

redesigned touching things always
numbering the codifications as a
clever craftswoman smirked Sigmund
mocked Flora laughed in

the center of voluptuousness

I paid a heavy debt here I found
the field of medicine down said
Leonardo pursing his lips artfully

the flows of his laying on of hand
cleansing the degenerated tissue away
examining the grim effects

the intense secrecy transforming
the stroke   symbol   cure
the sun would not have blazed nor

the trees greened the left corner
burnt her slow end of the century
lonely artist rocking
in a state of surprise

freeing her from outsight blood nerves
spaces between two bony areas

in this monograph of Lenny I write
it would be futile to blind ourselves

a young paysanne with smiling little
eyes reflecting in the pathological
circling mirror with smiling little
eyes diabolical artistic activity
explained her tightened eyelids

Leonardo frizzed his beard the edges a
worldwide complex aim to speak ill of
the living

it would be useful screaming standing
on a ladder the dizziness after this
funny moment of smirking

Lenny said a piece of senseless
impertinence to make a study of things
in him

that could just as easily be found in
the first person that one came across

Flora justifies her own version of
the fable as having for its aim an
attempt to explain something about
oil & bread

it seemed to her essential to say
something

floating in the atmosphere alone

nor is this way of knowledge

through a strange wood
decomposition breathing   sighed Mona
arched her wrists vigorously angling

with erect mistrust your notebooks
place them in sanctuaries stretch your
tongue curl the scrolls of thick veins
compositional thought

that led to a strange wood

stretched out arms a woman writhed
under the white throw exhaling molecular
breathing her fear bleeding

dressed as a traveler   confronts the
Sphinx of Sigmund divided into hundreds
of sections   the voice angling insatiable

vibrantly she unveils quickly she places

pushed forward breathing her fear bleeding
dressed as a paysanne the sinister

bones and carcasses lowered toward the
viewer

he describes the design sectioned into
depth and light cells skinlike tracing
the intent of Mona jumping forwards

talking outside about a forgery elegantly
painted that survived

the shock waves

a neutral din   your portrait I
tensed and didn't interact polychrome

wild bald eagles permitted to share
ragged & torn edges of the lake

Flora & Mona think strategically
you experimented beachcombing after
a storm searching

the woman covered with a white throw
nor is this way of knowledge unnatural
how the image of the wild bald eagles
superimposed on Lenny's white-blue

forehead rasping air nasal duplicated
I began to tear paper into strips
a background of fibers   textile imagery
she experimented with embedding bits
white mosaic stones the vigorous curve

of Lenny's dome wild bald eagles swarming
over the dumped rubble   you said it
had to be a forgery or a fake
that Lenny wore a peasant dress posing
as Mona but I say it is genuinely

Mona who posed artfully made up Flora

singing outside the atelier this afternoon
Flora was going to pose

I should not jump the gun
switching the vulture for the eagle
fatal caricatures learned step by step

the artifice of the canvas conspic-
uously flung risk & compulsion

chattered Mona of her early works
this afternoon Flora was going to
pose instead I turn the objects dead
wise around accuse lingering fueled
my artistic goal

how much the smile floats upon light
pushing

her strained thorax subtle color
simple keloid energy angling

slowly the molecular smile tenses
herself with herself brilliant

she interspersed in her scientific
heart-loneliness

a certain Caterina sniffed an art
historian probably a peasant girl
see her tightened eyelids
I turn relax my muscles
sodomize the account

widening the gap winked Lenny
blossoms of the sinuous motion hairs
on the wrists

outside the atelier

but then the boy's abdomen hot
I should not jump the gun

said I'm just beginning   believes
the order

I went again to the atelier
if this is true she reasons if this
is true   unknown to me searching myself
reading this breathing   changing a light
bulb magical significance

with a layer

tightening 'neath my shimmery hayre
and millions of manipulations

the base a granite stare Lenny's
stela copper tools placed lovingly
sealed the pit with a layer dirt
gypsum and stone rounded off another
grouping expanded and redesigned
I knew at first sight
Lenny brags

I was trying to decide what to do
next

she brags about her different reading
of what to do & what not to do

a mental wagging signal   flickerings
the merchant's wife

is the first person one came across
my first choice   simply the sound
of a fable

reworked felt wads of string   myself
that fit in exhaling
the dust on the covered hiding place

growth on Lenny's open desert
permitted rival theories a melancholy
scene   bones & carcasses undisturbed
stone splinters & dust past grows

blooms gathers significance searches
the seams reverberates my manic dream
of Mona superimposed

then seeks how the shroud was made
prolonged searching the atelier

& Mona seeing Munich's peasant flair
flushed the twofold riddle from her mind

dressed the boy defiantly wore greasy
lederhosen I have a drawing valid of her
filled with sausage & beer

like a contradictory current tricky
sleight of hand

holding her head to the side moving
the configurations smirking while some
artists sleep & dream of models
translated into life

your face looks back gently trembling
hair floats blossoms subtle color
a continuation dream of a young paysanne
her glance detached from space

expressing my own excavation & she let

you pose today like the young wife
of the Florentine merchant the deepening
folds of her dress exquisite

outside the infectious waste

you whispered ill of the dead
by origin of source Lenny stole a
discarded wallet

that you could focus the scene
of the vulture faithfully serving
fatal caricatures of Sigmund's

impertinence a volatile energetic
aggression toward the first person
you came across

throw those procedures open   you said
the smile of Gioconda floats upon

her features   you hook your neck
pursing your lips saturate your dry
eyelids with oil and very lightly

brush in this preherstory widening
your fibrous memory   this breathing
between random tasks sweeping the dust

enjoying company music showing off
touching your flushed Bacchus with soft
crossed thighs the familiar fascinating

heads of women who laugh

juxtaposed on your portrait fibrous
circles risk & compulsion your insatiable
facial nerves your mouth

ingratiating and subversive

Heaps of Heavy Stone

nor is this way of knowledge
unnatural for the flux insatiable
design without a law contradicts
the heaps of heavy stone felt the

tears of the boy bent forward   stretched
out both arms the sinister Lenny
folds & wrinkles scrolls of veins

And I thinking of that with bowed head
strayed from the main road that led
through a strange wood

degenerates   the child writhed and arched
his wrists backwards

the scrotum of the artist angling

his slow molecular orgasm

lazily you touch slowly you maneuver
accuse sodomize because it is not
the author's intent to write rectilinear
you have heard simply the songs
of dismemberment rasping sound of Lenny

breathing

Mona's eyes smile back cunningly
gnarled experimenting assessing the voice

watching my film scenario   draping a white
cloth the bleeding of the tot's anus
a pigeon stuffed into a niche
observed Mona   animali sighed Lenny

holding his head to the side

fueled accidental
and wearing my peasant dress gathered
puckered linen

I focused and photographed coldly
artful I who loved beauty that I always
trembled at the sight

see how he has made a breast of
his shoulders   because he wished to see
too far behind him   he looks behind
and makes his way backwards

Mona scrutinizes slowly measures numbers
See Lenny who changed semblance when
from male he became female transforming
all his members

and efforts of the hammer pounding my
arrangements isolated silently
you blamed my secrecy my hunger willful

I must make verses

into the fibers of the shroud the raw
data deviated redesigned left Lenny
pregnant and forlorn
& Sigmund seeing Munich's bestial
vapors
sorcerers we heard the neutral din

prolonged my numbering

the different substances reinforcing
your fixed image as in a photographic
negative

your fixed image forged worked feared

puzzling sudden intense blood stains
not the product from the power of
the pounding hammer   now Flora's face
is powdered with marble dust jovial &
happy not to sit for Lenny

just sit coldly she told Mona   he very
lightly gently brushes in the beautiful
colors

and the atelier in the darkness
and the sun would not have blazed nor
the trees become green nor Mona smirking

but I said a work is an accidental point
of leaving behind your first choice
nor is this way of the grouping
of energy & time of what to do
& what not to do

I went again to the atelier Flora brags
hooked my neck because I wished to see
backwards and gathered my peasant dress

Lenny scrutinized slowly mouthed

the image is an ongoing thirst

I have set before you   now feed
yourself

you were no more aware of Lenny's
inner cunning out of control stone
splinters and dust now his
face is smeared and powdered

gently he brushes in the beautiful
colors showing not by color
but by light

that sinister angling flickering
the edge geometrical

works to stamp her impulse smiled
Flora in a poetic mood see the holy
smile revolving roused up traces
of a useless numbering

ligament gray unraveling into dozens
of maneuvers I gently and very lightly

my love gallops sang Flora benignly
soft flap of the leather sandals

& bent forward   stretched out both arms
writhed and arched my wrists backwards

his glance detached from space

sketching the frontal view

and if our fantasies are low for such
a loftiness

in no dark sayings

you pose today like the young wife
of the Florentine merchant

in the atelier
exactly 4 o'clock my body oriented

I'm a hungry bum searching the seams
of a discarded wallet
quietly muttering

sealing the fate of Lenny
tightening a light bulb scrutinized
the expanded grouping 4 corners maneuvers
riddle of random devastation
views burning mistrusts the details

and wearing my peasant dress saw
the dead woman lying in the street
holding her head to the side
coldly I preserve her notebooks

having all the facts of the young wife
of the Florentine merchant

I saw Lenny in the light
I had torn a fragment & analyzed
see me going from the center to the end
of the century

You noted listened your slanting mouth
fabricated authorship

nor Flora early in the morning
diligently manipulating

my work into Mona's work then seeks
how the shroud was made

felt wads of string my patch of scalp
seven fine sutures

projected slides showed how in less
than a century   the face of a stone

angel squeezing his eyes shut
was disfigured by vibration the ceiling
in the atelier and Mona's titillating
discovery converging opening her hand
revealing the image swarming with

things twice dead darted wonder at me

And Mona continuing Lenny's discourse
mouthed the image is an ongoing thirst
had she not been intent on another
strange thing

for through the middle of a photographic
negative your face

which once I wept for dead

while the boy chewed up hazel-nuts
spitting them out in her hand

& Mona happy to sit for Lenny while he
very lightly brushes against her
hooked his neck because he wished to see
backwards

the pace of the work broken edges dozens
of white mosaic stones V-shaped in black
stone the ceiling in the atelier

sanctified scrutinized Mona touching

reflecting in the window glass when
Sigmund focused backwards so shall you
hear how my buried flesh ought

to have moved you
I should not jump the gun you startle
yourself watching Sigmund's eyes artful
& coy I suddenly interrupt myself

no more will I say and I know that I
speak darkly making up the stories about
Flora falsely contributing mutterings
moaning about two versions corrupting
the pristine expanse transfixed

an arc of sticks begins to crumble
Flora liked to bring the brat to torment
her tormentor

strange sweet odor as he solidly squats
and tortures his cute packed lederhosen
heating up Lenny so that cellular locations
press against

the scrotum of the artist angling
Lenny cried that he loved beauty that
I always trembled at the sight & Flora
happy to sit for Lenny & Lenny happy
while she very lightly holds her head
to the side squeezing her eyes shut

her slow molecular orgasm
and the atelier in the darkness
her face is powdered with marble dust

so that she looks like a baker

diverted and collide sent through
a strange wood blocks of the universe
when the universe was 0.00000000000001
seconds old

nor is this way of how the portrait
fabricating the smile of Gioconda

using your features   I hook my neck
watching any of the thousand and one
particles

on the formation of Mona's inner life
roused up like a wild beast

not a single line of Lenny's sketches
betrays my fibrous memory   this breathing
between random tasks I came across

besides the picture is a portrait
defining itself on the fabric
the last of the onion after all else

is peeled pulled along the portrait
consuming your facial nerves forward
stretched out my numbed arms in the space
of Mona's atelier

mistrusts his notebooks riddle of
the white throw   14 feet   3 inches
long 3 feet   7 inches wide   bears faint
hidden forms   bears the origin of source

slowly snow falling   see Mona going
that sinister fixed smile

on elongated sinuous lips

I can no longer do without
Lenny says   I am left with less than

comfort before my work
he gently and very lightly brushes
in the beautiful colors
And he is left with less than one drop
of her blood

the degree of suspicion between himself
and his contemporaries

I who know her from her numbed arms
in the space of the atelier

see how she beats her breast there
so shall you hear how my buried flesh
ought to have moved you

& bent backwards you pose today
then seeks how the accidental point
alone   the folds of the dress spatial
see the tensed arched foot
I should not jump the gun

you had this curious conception of
a beaming jovial and happy Lenny

image of a whipped and crucified
woman smashing converging numbering
the codifications trusts her black art
guiltless Flora ought to have posed
but Mona is my friend

see how she has made the fibers

structuring patiently

I clamp the fragments through
sophisticated orders
and a little varnish and oil
constant exhaling I say my name
Da Vinci swells the brushwork hears
the burning spelt out a shift toward
thicker traces of edges screws
destabilizes the enigma

that sinister fixed smile insect
parts segmented stretched out my numbed
arms

in the space of the atelier writhed
and arched backwards you beat your
breast there

then seeks how the shroud was made
echoing his mistrust because she wished
to see backwards consuming the portrait
spitting it out in his hand

the pace of the work diverted
Flora said Mona's just sitting here

see Mona going

that sinister fixed smile consuming
your inner collapse

sectioned into depth and light cells
the intent of Lenny jumping forwards
pulled along the portrait

head down   then backwards she looks
in the space of the atelier searching
for her shoes

that is Leonardo's portrait corrupting
serving fate by the flourish of the leaves
evaluated Mona but the cycle of painting
disintegrating

stare coldly Lenny said in a poetic mood

look like a Spanish princess
and wearing my peasant dress chanted
Flora a woman on the loose

strange kinds of repetitive sinuous
depths into dozens of broken edges

the body of my sounds with molecular
enlarging

rose like a column of blood
tensed the heart wall one upon one gaps
in the pattern filled with white noise
gaps in the history of Mona's life

disappeared
Flora was going to pose but Mona is
her friend

in the presence of a smirking cracked
statue you sit eating white beans
watching the boy snake-dance towards
the hiding place

Swaddled in Guiltless Lederhosen

breathe erode capricious playing
the boy opened his mouth

Lenny is covered with small marble
splinters so that it seemed that it
snowed on his back Flora said poetically
watching the boy

you break into joy singing watching
I'm a hungry bum searching the seams
of a discarded wallet
my body superimposing itself dozens
into depths the passage from

the hiding place
she put the lukewarm salt water into
the cup of her hand slowly you mesmerize
underpay the apprentices & hotly stare

his heart-shaped heinie swaddled
in guiltless lederhosen

while numbering the sounds of my body
in the space of the atelier
Flora was looking for her shoes

a lira here a lira there

that the hefty brat had hidden
found a box of eye-paint with three
stolen golden chains

gratification of the active twisting
brat

which once I wept for dead
while the boy chewed up hazel-nuts

rotating his tense abdomen
artfully infected with play crawling

under the coarse folds of Leonardo's
smock

with that persistence Mona's system

her eyes look around

when she could examine a big part
of the whole   you fear for your death
memory flaking bones loosened screaming
tightening 'neath my shimmery hayre
exhaling repeating prayers in Latin

Leonardo's slow molecular orgasm

a lira here a lira there
he was seized with a feeling of pathos
whence does that arise

the breath brush pivoting on the master's
scrotum

inserting fatal caricatures of Lenny
you said

the intense diagnostic revenge
of the merchant's wife smirked Sigmund
to make a study of things in him

that could just as easily be found

in the first person one came across

He triumphantly smiled on reading
a pathological review of a great man

a lira here a lira there

loosened the voluptuous center traced
the wife of the Florentine la Gioconda
I worked for years on the portrait
spasmodically
until twilight never thinking of
eating or drinking

and did not put the brush out of my
hand

I say just do it coldly

peasant dress & slanting smile
bitter earwax in the cleft slowly
the liquid filters through

a lira here a lira there

giggled Leonardo animali sighed Flora

a lira here a lira there
& turning the multiple drawings of Mona
set on fire the cellular details
into compulsive dots

depths cracked segmented a little
varnish and oil shifting your mistrust

& bent backwards Mona poses today

you are left with less than comfort
before her work
so shall you hear how my buried flesh
ought to have moved you

In order to draw she remained for
hours worked for years diverting
the number of sketches

and did not leave the brush out
of her hand till twilight
with the brush to add a few strokes
without putting her hand on it

never thinking of here nor there

she always trembled when she began
to paint

the final flight of the blood
smirked Flora

while sounding the numbers of my body
a lira here a lira there

an embodiment fueled accidental
on the face of it   done coldly the dots
icy the piles of debris higher
than the hiding place an arc of sticks
if I thought that two fires

Mona chanted walled in the pattern
filtering slowly he liked to fault
segmented enlarging two versions

one upon one gradual dense
I should not jump the gun
a lira here a lira there

winters are long in Vinci gently she
brushes in the despised smile fibrous
circles the burnt left edge

and soon divines

my book breaking into parts

it seemed that I always trembled
was as little due to her uncompleted
works the stain due to reasoning
compulsively whetting the boy's
palate

that a photographic negative
during the year of Leonardo's birth
bony between spaces you focused
traced the fragment

that unfathomable   smile always with
water white mosaic stones to force
the cycle increase the pathological
degree

I became a close friend

me as a clever craftswoman coldly
underpaying the apprentices
a lira here a lira there
such wish-fantasies pursing fibrous

the smile of Gioconda screws in these
unfavorable times   stretched out my
numbed arms in the space of Lenny's
life

when the universe was 0.00000000000001
seconds old mistrusts your notebooks
betrays my sinuous lips consuming using
my features   you hook your neck watching
any of the random tasks

To others you fault like me

who was absorbed
the flows codified burned artfully
clever craftswoman I cared more and more
spending intentional the passing on

of a message from Lenny to Mona

a lira here a lira there
full of gaps and full of lights foresight
disorderly bundles

and that it bears the logic unmarked
the absence unfinished

I worked for years bent forward

human animali power loosened beyond
diversion pivoting on the master's
scrotum

doubling the versions slowly before her
revenge on reading glances backward
viewed

in the end of a pathological review
of a great man

a lira here a lira there
gathering tightening breaking my book
into parts segmented depths cracked

I say just do it coldly

twice some of the past implanted

A Lira Here a Lira There

slowly doubling the space slowly
exhaling bent forward I worked for
years filtering segmenting

even adding smegma

in the gaps sinking in filling in
she gently and very lightly brushes
in the beautiful colors

see Mona between herself and her
contemporaries

with small marble splinters so that
it seemed as if it snowed on her back
a lira here a lira there

winters are long in Vinci
when she was scrutinizing the precise
texts deadly pebbles in the female breast

segmenting Lenny's inner collapse
smegma when he was giving vent circling
in rage around the twisting brat

which once I wept for dead
& forcing my rolling shoulders pulled back
the foreskin

a fold of the artist's smock
in the space of the atelier
a lira here a lira there beyond diversion

your eyes look around my buried flesh
swelling patterned

image of the front and back of
a female breast this suspicion
scrutinizing scourge marks

and blood stains impulse thrown off
three-dimensionality

your brightness in variations
smegma sinking in the gaps slowly
the decay

Mona left only some anatomical drawings

a lira here a lira there

light and heat into the text
the front and back brush pivoting
on the master's scrotum accused
exhaling he bent forward

numbering the scourge marks and blood
stains she bent backwards rolling
segmenting grasping radiated light

when she began to lay to rest faults
to make a study of things
which once you wept circling two

versions forbidden smegma in the pattern

the solution consuming the cycle
the smile of Gioconda using my features
you became a clever craftswoman

a lira here a lira there

gathering the multiple drawings
of Lenny sighed Mona shifting varnish
in the cleft slowly

disintegrating the suspicion replaced
the manacles resting on the heap of
marble dust a geometric pattern

hexagons white mosaic forbidden in

devices diagnostic tools Mona learned

what evidence grasped only in one way
the smile of your features

a brat of evil repute see him snake-dance
across the floor Lenny runs up saying
a lira here a lira there reverberating
running down the opulent decor

from east to west you say in a lyrical
tone transfixed by a drawing of the
position of the floating uterus

drawn by Lenny when still a child
stained with a fiery signature reddish
pattern little Lenny could be brought

up in his father's house

I should not jump the gun but Mona
said there was no sign of only one
version

to make a study of things

a lira here a lira there
I say just do it coldly to others
the unfinished absence ought to have
moved you

that could just as easily be found
in the first person

the place where we came
those livid reds

the eyes possess that moist luster
a lira here a lira there   and that
it bears to her insult fetal clicks

the opening of the mouth with its
red ends
sneaking between Mona and Lenny
the brat runs up to your feet and
solidly sits down backwards

winters are long in Vinci you said
smiling through bullet-proof glass

lightly brushes in the beautiful colors

yellows the varnish and alters the pigment

see Flora between herself and her
contemporaries

segmenting your red ends doubling
scrutinizing my versions halfway across
the atelier

I'm gathering the drawings rolling

light and heat into the text

you exhaust the procedure it seems
that she always trembled when she
detected faults in those things
which appeared wonderful to others

exhaling you bent backwards
along the dark rock on this side
and on that

I turn my mind to what I saw
and I curb my genius more than I am wont

done coldly Lenny chanted diverted he
worked for years bent forward even

adding smegma ever-versatile artistic
and commercial imagination
each swathes herself with that which
burns her

I became a close friend gathering you
became a clever craftswoman inserting
light and heat into the text

androgynous impulse ransacked
the author's century   it dawns suddenly

unearthed my work into stone splinters
you stare holding your head to the side

and wearing your peasant dress sunlight
changes isolated silent

she always trembled at the sight

two upon two dense gradual
codifying slowly you maneuver water
sugar salt artful oblivious squirts
juice felt the vomit of the boy

which once I wept for dead
Flora said in a poetic mood I made
the flame appear more glowing

inhaling we bent forward colors
in those things those livid reds

on this side and on that

I look to everyone the same
you have seen the home of Mona
she's ever-versatile in a backdrop
he paid a heavy debt behold him
they mistrust me

artfully making up my eyes so
I watched Lenny when he was

giving vent in the space segmenting

beyond diversion angling during days
of sitting ensnaring melted geometric
vibratory the nether hell

a lira here a lira there that could

just as easily be found

winters are long in Vinci the old
versions disintegrating altered
the pigment

lightly brushes in the beautiful colors
on this side and on that

where he falsified flowing blackening
she worked for years even adding smegma
thickened the reddish lids the cloven
tail hidden in the folds of the dress
bunched the member that man conceals

squatted down petted the writhing brat

which once I wept for dead

so that already the load down there
is heavy upon me

with Mona's double nature as an artist
and investigator
squeezing his eyes shut and wearing
his smock he worked for years his throat
of travail exhaling from azure to white

overflowing sectioned the fetal clicks
slight slow insult forbidden   two versions

and with my shadow I made the flame

appear more glowing

lightly brushes in the beautiful colors

I made the flame appear more glowing

light and heat into the text the smile
of Gioconda said Mona in a poetic mood
inhaling she bent forward transfixed
by a drawing of the position of

the floating uterus

drawn by Lenny when still a child
to her insult to make a study of things

now I see the net that entangles you here
exhaling Flora bent backwards listening
to your bitter sighs reddish pattern
fetal clicks overflowing   insults

my buried flesh ought to have moved you

with what is unknown

burns light to powder traces
inserts the details of my life

betrayed by fraud fueled slowly
with what is inhaled sniffed Lenny
squeezing his tube of lup-pud
experimenting he turns the brush
slowly motions sinuously swathes

reds the ooze backwards up transcribes
the smegma to the portrait comes across
his biography accidentally

and if her fantasies are my dark
sayings details his mistrust

then seeks how the shroud was made

a lira here a lira there

folds her cloven tail that burns
her   unearths all his members
prolongs the latest lament Flora's
long & pessimistic poem

I should not jump the gun

holding the tube of paint soaking
beyond the portrait moon-gray fibers
reworked changing layers numbers

stone & gypsum redesigns fits
himself with that which he came
across

with what is known

escaped vibratory the history
of Leonardo's life maneuvering

light and heat into the text

a lira here a lira there

which once I wept for dead
isolated silent behold the woman

my face is powdered with marble dust
so that I look like a baker

I chose oil colors the drying of
which permitted me to complete
the picture according to my mood
and leisure

winters are long in Vinci strange
fatal testimonies

he stole the money from my purse
a lira here a lira there
only definite information edges
the sound of my body forward

transfixed she looks in the space
insatiable

in Mona's picture Lenny sits on
Flora's lap bent forward and stretching
out both arms

that peculiar luster breathing
backwards to the past sitting
ensnaring one upon one gaps

to her insult fetal clicks overflowing
his throat charred horizontal timber
the numerous vessels of the remains
of cremations

but Flora said there was no sign of
only two versions while intertwining
the codifications

the brat runs up to Lenny's feet
solidly sits down backwards

his heart-shaped heinie swaddled
in guiltless lederhosen

burning forcing the outlines patterned
beyond diversion which once I wept for
in the space of the atelier for years

she worked molecular the twofold image
could not have blazed angling sinister
sectioned into fibrous circles

which once I wept for dead

he filtered for years segmenting even
adding smegma winters are long in Vinci
inhaling she bent forward and very

lightly brushes in the beautiful colors
the back and front image

see Flora between Mona and Lenny
circling in the darkness arched

to the side squeezing her eyes shut
and wearing my peasant dress Lenny said
in a poetic mood

that the anonymous scribe was

by fraud betrayed

but Mona indicated that the
long & pessimistic poem about
the place where we came

inhaling I bent forward my unknown

earlier lament circling codifying
smegma sugar salt continuing those

things which appeared wonderful
reds livid those eyes creating
a fake ooze out of the portrait beyond
the obscure details of your life

each swathes herself with that which
burns her   exhaling Lenny solidly sits
down backwards inserting traces
shimmering the lup-pud of the paint

oft times I am like a woman by fraud
betrayed

you had come to light your face is
powdered and smeared lazily Flora
transcribed

Lenny's biographer pursing her lips

squeezing her eyes shut and brushing
her smock lightly brushes in the beautiful
faults a rim of the paint tube

with what is known

a lira here a lira there

smiling yellows those livid reds
rolling the drawings

on this side and on that
her versions scrutinized segmented
grimaced
a lira here a lira there
she worked for years inserting
opening her eyes of travail

unearthed her ends ransacked
the place where we came

her whitish crossed gnarled foot

which could just as well be found
in every Tom Dick & Harry
penetrate useless bacteria
and mold

wipe out the location the open
storerooms winters are long in Vinci
but Flora said that the long poem
appeared wonderful the portrait moved

beyond the obscure details

of Lenny's life

I'm gathering the drawings rolling
light & heat into the text
oft times I am like a woman by fraud
betrayed smeared the lup-pud

of the paint
I worked for years tracing bent forward

over the versions

I pressed forward unfinished
the slowness with which Lenny
worked and did not leave the wet

brush out of my hand

I will set my hand to color it

through you I was a poet
deviated the raw data designed
I must make my hand to color it
coldly artful

and the atelier in the darkness

I must make verses

into the fibers of the shroud
white lead out of my hand fluid

tilted both her palms fixed and
stained he learned from her devices

dropping your left hand stroking
reverberating fixing his eyes on
her patch of scalp

wretched on the shreds of the work
which to your own hurt was wrought
by Mona's strained thorax

quickened the maneuvers the corner
congested light broken in front
it seemed that she always trembled
when she braided her hair

Flora Was Going to Pose

One substance in three persons
that the cycle a rhythmic compulsion
I could not put the brush

out of my hand   heat & light
you made shadow creating her
design and bent her brow repeating
her own name

to give sinuous hairs vibration
under the coarse brown felt

the vomit of the boy

I turned to my side fearing
that I was abandoned when you
saw the ground darkened before

me only

our face looks posed like a young
paysanne trembling in itself

and the deep wounds of the dead
woman her burning hair details
collapse flies to the end
of her notebooks valve clicks
scratched Lenny's name in the
register of the members

Flora was going to pose but Mona
is her friend clamps her hand on
the edge of the masterpiece squeezed
the wet brush lightly smeared

the lup-pud exhaling Lenny bent
forwards

This course semi-circular drawn

over your shoulder discovers I
posed like a young paysanne

a sketch drawn in the atelier

but then embraced him singing
she unearths the gold chains
that the brat had hidden

shifting her hip see the withdrawing
dismemberment

three stolen golden chains
a lira here a lira there

I worked for two days my long
gray hands collected and sifted

spawned this aberration sifted all
available fragments stuck in
the vulture-phantasy juxtaposed
maneuvered

subtle color through your light brown
hayre seven days sitting in the midst
a lira here a lira there

his slow molecular orgasm

Lenny's biographer swathing herself
salt sugar smegma to light your
face squeezing a rim of the paint

by fraud betrayed the obscure details

his mother was a certain Caterina

he saw himself pure down ancient
in his cradle deciphered trusting
gently into the poem of the white
cloth
as Mona's Leonardo felt tightening
behind the veil she attempted to
fill the gaps in the cremains

I edged past your masterpiece
your pale & gasping son

let me pose today Flora intoned

bears faint hidden forms

bears the final & cynical rupture
between art & money propped backwards

a lira here a lira there

work quickly while the foreground
is still moist isolated painted
she chose colors the drying of which

permitted her to complete the picture
according to my mood & leisure

the cremains in the gaps settle
and separate themselves float up
her nose itching

& Lenny happy to sit for Flora

while she very lightly defines
into light & depth

you beat your breast there sitting
exhaling patiently structuring

went singing and culling flower
from flower with which all her
path was painted

agitating the model's double-
jointed crossed gnarled foot

but Flora said Mona gathers that
which conceals nothing she must
make verses into the shroud maneuvers
the darkness coldly artful

then to the fair lady I turned
my face I passed the edge of
the masterwhole my breast itching
rapt reader cracked depths sifted
grains fueled the articulate fetus
exhaling

while slowly you startle while
slowly I depict the icy dots
of the spiritual condition

the sun would not have blazed
nor the trees become green nor
Mona smirking Lenny sticking
the dead woman's sewing needle
into a ball of felt a longing

the vomit of the brat spreading
sweetness

claimed devotion years after
the shroud appeared devotion woven
into the coarse brown felt fragments
layered the seams

my work into Mona's work unearthed

And if my discourse does not appease
your hunger

flakes from my bones
which once you wept for dead
winters are long in Vinci the yellow
smegma traces   it seemed that he

always trembled when he began
to dissect

the background   still moist

the image front and back details
of the merchant's wife Sigmund came
across on reading a pathological

review of a great man segmented
inserting grains of salt patterned

and transmuted fueled accidental
whole is my will

and it would be wrong to act against
its pleasure

a lira here a lira there

my long gray hands sifted depths
cracked

I made the flame appear more glowing

and backed against with what is
unknown

had she been silent

strip off the slough reader
rapt turned to my side one rocks
in front sounds your versions
which could just as well

be found in every Tom Dick
& Harry

and showed me a wound high on
Lenny's breast weeping pits
her foot crossed with whitish
cremains her left hand dropping
downward beyond

the obscure details of Mona's
life closing stained her hand
smoothing the coarse brown felt
the brush smear the lup-pud

reverberating faint hidden forms

you pressed forward worked

your face which once I wept for
dead opening coldly the storerooms
ransacked after the fire

beneath the dismembered cadaver
infected perfection he feared
the second fire burns so near

that you understand what you sing

beyond the obscure details
wrought by a flirtatious peasant
girl

pale breasts a gift Lenny intoned
traces a flame of my discourse which

appeared wonderful to others

Mona's intimate life meager biography
wrought slowly perforated brushed
grouped my life & age downward cremains

I'm a hungry bum searching the seams
of a discarded wallet

look our slanting mouths the tightened
midline sounds her versions rigors of
my docudrama you arch your foot your
eyes small & hard & round with disgust

And if my discourse does not appease
your hunger into the veins going unknown
a cup of gold infectious waste reddish
hair of Lenny

guarding the deepening folds of the dress

the aging master in a frenzy shook
the lederhosened brat of Flora
and he had to strike the facial nerve

whose enigmatic smile came out of a
skin suture

Flora cried a boy on the loose
she imitated simply let   her pose
as the smirking paysanne

and she had to strike the facial
nerve

they built the city over those
dead bones for to that alone does
Mona's mind revert scattered around

America the cruel virgin said Lenny
in a poetic tone the old master felt
a longing my love gallops
a lira here a lira there circular
intoned Flora let   me pose today
I worked forward her pressed discourse

cracked and backed against with what
is discovered silent the boy sifted
grains into the eyes of the rapt
reader moist the background glowing

traces smegma a flame of yellow sang
Lenny
And if my discourse does not appease
your hunger
sifted grains fueled the articulate
fetus layered the fragments into
the coarse brown felt

I brushed the work the lup-pud
reverberated beyond the obscure details
of my palms

segmenting filtering beyond diversion
vent in rage circling the precise
photographic negative

there grains beneath his left
hand moving upward downward as you
smear the lup-pud balancing perfection

hidden forms unbalanced unforeseen
Mona's breast weeping pits your
cremains active shoot fall trace
the outlines of the portrait shaft
the ovum   spermatozoon blood

filtering myself as I always was
said Lenny who deigned to set your
hand to writing our lifetask

when she began to paint the image
back and front side turned her
versions beyond the obscure details

felt the faults

it seems that she always trembled
when she began to paint

dismembered the cadaver set
the horns of the cross

the head & neck of a vulture patterned
in the fire dragged down cracked
depths of the atelier

Mona intoned my discourse
I'm a hungry bum searching the seams
of a discarded wallet

felt the facial nerve circular
glowing

and Lenny isolated the blissful
smile sucking in cool air Flora
intoned repeating

a longing my love gallops unveils
the cruel virgin artfully polychromed
pale breasts upward downward breath

of the Florentine merchant's wife
come from her mirror with unpainted
face

were I to smile a longing fragmenting
her versions from one unbroken day
I worked my long gray hands forward
blindingly fast

felt the faults sharp cracked shining
before you only in the depths of
the atelier beyond the edge
of the masterwhole

America the cruel virgin intoned
Mona   my love gallops over dead bones
scattered around

the white skin turns black felt
her left hand patterned in the fire
silvered the skin suture the ends
reversed negative

image of a whipped and crucified
woman

darkened after me only and Lenny had
to strike the facial nerve

illumination that she detected
how the shroud was made rapt your
face which once I wept for
dead he loved beauty

that he always trembled at the sight
silver brocade trimmed velvet
I saw thin layers the fragment
traced my skin suture

the breath in the cloth of your
caricature the pleasure in the worms
beneath the dismembered cadaver

Lenny who loved beauty that he always
trembled my love gallops Lenny said
in a poetic tone America the cruel
virgin Mona intoned brushed the lup-pud

downward upward felt the faults
unforeseen grains smeared the horns

felt the facial nerve glowing

my face which once you wept for dead
Mona who posed artfully polychromed
breasts pale you arch your foot

crossed with whitish cremains
he unveils quickly and showed me

a wound the shredded riddle searching
the transparent sketch nervous

image of a whipped and crucified
woman

You shut off your emotions
the sinister Lenny sang smoothing
the brat's feverish head
squeezed leaves from the onion

plant behind the mound of ashes
sit coldly you said suck in your
cheeks

sit wondering in the same position
one can sit wondering in the same
position in blinding rains
thinks Mona nailed into space
rolling up her notebooks felt
the coarse grains perforating

her feverish skin
the child came with the south wind

peasant dress and slanting smile
the vomit of the brat spreading
sweetness

then to fair Flora's itching
breast Lenny smirking

look our slanting mouths went
singing and culling flower from
flower

the menstrual lup-pud into the fibers
fixed blackening flows upward downward

Lenny bent forwards

on her hip and looks down
mysterious and sinister swarms
of mosquitoes Mona's impulse
spatial

felt the silky clots and the second
just to the east of the atelier
I depict the icy dots between
random tasks   a lira here a lira
there

that a photographic negative glowing
a gift pale breasts intoned Lenny

see the rapt reader going

in the space of the enigma
you put the lukewarm salt water into
the cup of your hand

pudenda Lenny smirked smegma whispered
Flora made up Sigmund shifting
your mistrust

I say just do it coldly between
any of the random tasks

that smile breaking into parts
hexagons stained with a fiery signature
then seeks how the shroud was made

I should not jump the gun
Lenny's biographer pursing his lips

scratched Mona's name searching
the seams

widening the gap

you edged past pressing the circles

a lira here a lira there
to strip her body after death
on this side and on that altered
the hidden contours

of Mona's raw data
but then the boy's abdomen tensed
he very lightly brushes the deepening
suture silvers the ends isolates

his blissful smile

artfully assaults the three-fold
image past the edge which weeps
striking the facial nerve

she worked for two days her rapt
face at one instant looking
simultaneously on this side

and on that he brushed the work
the lup-pud shining

because Mona's blackening
the caricature was the cyclic flow
the menstrual lup-pud into the fibers

fluid fixed the flame fragmented
intoned Flora

she edged livid pursing his lips
defining herself on the fabric

and Mona's montage meeting
in the middle
the book of my words and the book

of horses see her going from
the center embodying spatial flesh

comfort me with treachery   the air
is full with grace and sweetness

comfort me with pornography
enlarging abundant great rains

And an old man only a few hours
before he died told me that he had
lived for one hundred years

you passed the brat while he sketched
and numbered using Lenny's black
and red pencil   your patch of scalp
monstrously drawn by my ardent

desire   Flora's eyes scrutinized
curving her glance shown in a drawing
in one form all the details flayed
versed the energy of the articulate
fetus and the fruiting plant

deliberately worked slow cellular
the cracks in the stones optical
stitching the white cloth

so that his cute heinie garbed
in lederhosen so sturdy he is resembles
the curve of a valentine heart

I let you pose today stretched
the canvas tightly   on the shreds
coldly artful

and the atelier in the darkness
quickened you bent forwards stroking
absorbed fueled Leo na r do

it seems that she always trembled
when she braided her hair

the painful perfection merely
passed through chiaroscuro from
the deep wounds degenerative bitter
dug-up squirts of red or black
unforeseen

and Lenny isolated the blissful
smile shining before you only

my eyes small & hard & round with
disgust intoned for the pleasure
of being

And if my discourse does not appease
your hunger state of suspicion
you arch your foot moving my life
& age

silvered the skin suture
isolated   my verses from one
unbroken day Flora intoned laced
her fingers in the dismembered
cadaver

stained the bony branching cross-
sectional folds rhythms rapacious
textures thinks Mona nailed into space

dilating the numbered text warped
the rectilinear opening

she always trembled when she began
to paint

dismissed me as a clever craftswoman
superimposing you angled your version
sketched during secular week your
portrait sphinctered virile

Lenny giggled   with the hard
teeth of old age saying

I played with a conscious and virtuoso
hand

Flora sat with water studies
revolving with crossed gnarled recto
and verso stimulus forms of the bones

Flora who loved to pose as the smirking
paysanne the brat on her hip and looks
down

see the reader going rapt in the space

your mistrust of her notebooks your
pursing sinister giggled Mona smegma-
lips

Sigmund segmented me using my black
and red pencil bent forwards in
the space of the atelier

picture level unrolls the topsoil
cracked pottery in the space
of the atelier

inscriptions in Latin strata striations
the cremains in the gaps gently into
the poem went singing and culling
from dissection to dissection

Mona saying she was a hidden
caricature wrought by a flirtatious
peasant girl scratching her ankle

limbs surrounded by frequent folds
and swirling about these limbs
she worked her long gray hands
her own experiments stimulated by
contact float up angling his body
dozens of apertures measurements
perpetual

fastened to the wheel Lenny argues
says that Mona's drawn indented
raised & descended across space
felt a longing

I edged past your masterpiece
your pale & gasping son

as Flora's veil absorbed smoke air
and dust

covered bearing jagged semi-liquid
geometrical grace

And I Made an Anatomy to See

four rows hexagons splashing
the corners bunching her bodice
up

a tender wet-nurse I turned my face
then to fair Flora's itching breast
bitter coralline fruit red pale
yellowish painted traces of
the useless dissection

the sacrificed uterus

a line of swirls the sharp arithmetical
measures burning the portrait's left
corner exhaling I turn the portrait
around protein sugar salt water

a mirror of fire sang Lenny benignly
the muscles two versions at dusk
& at night searching the foreground
opening

for it comes to my mind
I'm a hungry bum searching the seams
of a discarded wallet

your mistrust of her notebooks
suspicion laced the canvas coldly
artful

numbered the umbilical cords simply
heard the songs of dismemberment
transposes Mona into surgeon after
the expulsion

And I made an anatomy to see
the cause of a death so sweet

I turned to my side fearing
that I was abandoned scratched
Mona's future nailed into space

my dissection of a child of two
years in which I found everything
to be opposite old age

I edged past the cracks of
stones darkened your floating
uterus illuminated the praying
gesture coldly artful layered
the hair scalp lactarious flesh
reversed the ends

your pale & gasping son with bared
teeth

the black skin turns white and if
you can draw me posed like me only
behind the veil within the earth
and outside it before you detected
faults

the brat's vomit spreading sweetness

Mona's desire remorseless to codify

You worked for two days your long
gray hands collected and sifted

blazed divided the circumference only
painting only deviated plundered bursts
inward gasping darkened the vomit

the vomit spreading sweetness I edged
past my death the light as a million
parts tricky you moved coldly artful
reverse fold of the tunic vented

her uterus floating into space
your pale & gasping son angled recto

slits life-size screamed Lenny white
faults turned air against air the fœtal
soul simpered Lenny

his slow molecular orgasm
days you can draw me left to right
stretched the portrait worked
the hexagons distill the vortex

If anything was ever done tell me?
I played with a conscious and virtuoso
hand

segmented the water layered chilling
the dark rays with dead water segmented
remorseless

your pale & gasping son undescribed
your Sigmund passes from behind
the vertebrae the brat's face turned
smoke & dust & flames ends the forms

You worked for two days your long
gray hands collected and sifted obscure
faults

scratched obscure details three
blocks writing you were outlines
origins said Mona poignantly fire

my crucified palms nailed into space

whispered Sigmund breaking into parts

a lira here a lira there see rapt
reader going intoning

to strip inlines enlarge melting
atelier from one unbroken day

forms surface cadaver

pits unbalanced fingers joints fluid
your blissful smile your face rapt
splashed by swollen dissection
flesh layered arrangements

culled buds leaves writing book
her words book horses see Flora going
from center embodying spatial flesh

it seems that she always trembled
when she began to paint

yellow water studies Flora my own
sketches superimposing opening

portrait smirking paysanne

I worked brush sectional branching
your piece discourse culling singing
songs dismemberment

forging America the cruel virgin
galloping behind the fragments

edged sifted very lightly you
played with a conscious and virtuoso
hand opening vessels rhythm

of her raw data depths cut dessicated
ebb and flow Mona intoned the spout

spiritual parts you remind yourself
tricky sleight of hand

then seeks how the shroud was made
neck of the aorta and Flora argues
that it is forced in part to turn back
on itself in a spiral motion

extends going from her hand glances
at the thumbnail sketch draws back
witness the rapt reader going

your blissful smile nailed into space

revert see there pits surface folds
her tunic 'neath my head

slits life-size screamed Lenny
the old master felt a longing she brushed
the lup-pud rays of the hexagons your
pressed discourse

mute one anatomy after the other your
uterus floating on blank pages Flora
crooned

Lenny left-handed dilated the text
studied your sinister fibers fixed
sketches of splashing

coldly artful when the experimenter
slows freezes the mutilations
engages now   stops Mona's isolation
recycles the rhythm

I had to do it like this so that
the birds could sing

drawing the musculature
a body of sculpture the beauty is
screwed together embedded mental
mortal Flora crooned

a trachea whence the voice passes
b œsophagus whence the food passes
c apoplectic vessels whence pass
the vital spirits
d dorsal spine where the ribs arise
e vertebrae where the muscles arise
which end in the neck and raise up
the face to the sky

your pale & gasping Sigmund segmented
the unknown contours of the atelier
apart splashing a cold solution
Flora attempted to inflate a pig's
lung

You turn the portrait around segment
your slow molecular orgasm squeezing

drawing you posed like me sweetness
of the vomit of the brat   she cracked
depths diversion beyond numbers scratched
Lenny's name on the edge of the master

hole

the unknown contours thrust her
thumbnail distorted exiled nor was
there space another poses in a trance

truncated less and less Mona O with
limbs scattered across your biography

fingered the alchemists searched
the traces forged the sketches bent
twisted the muscles the overall shape
matching behind part one of Lenny's
desiring pricking the portrait

your pale & gasping son
for it comes to my mind I'm a hungry
bum searching the seams wrung and
bled out licking the vertebrae

my turned face rent your fear lactarious
screwed one style into another
embedded the rhythm your sinister
fibers nailed behind dissection

of a child with her throat cut
see how the text erects the flight
breaking Sigmund into parts segmenting

your pale & gasping son fair Flora
fingers the veil white faults turned
the brat upside-down spreading

coldly artful slowly you depict the
icy dots of the spiritual condition
his slanting mouth opened

so that his cute heinie garbed in

lederhosen so sturdy he is resembles
the curve of a valentine heart

tunic folds behave like skin
Flora said inside the germination
blending functional 'neath my shimmery
hayre my head 'neath her name

knowledge Leo na r do much how
one part may be visible behind
the other and then make one

you are about to say something
about oil & bread

from behind

dissection of a boy with his throat
cut you look at the floating uterus
two follicles crossed the verso
of this sketch the sun and thumbnail
sketches of the sketches of Mona

nailed into space

And I made an anatomy to see
the cause of a death so sweet

the flap one plane into another
verging details imitating a spider
on a mirror smirking we posed
on-center outer shutting highly
that the core is whole life-size
drawing slits erected

a beautiful male Lenny screamed
squaring his shoulders and rolling
his tunic up into a ball

clasped the brat thievish in
my throat when you sat beside her

fear in splinters paint glare saw

the chain clubbed stained pages
ransacked philosophy

obstacles do not bend me every obstacle
is destroyed through rigor
Sigmund segmented plagued still in
the cradle unswerving
giggled Lenny tightly stretched
the foreskin inflated the testicle

coldly artful trembled Flora saying
I played with a conscious and virtuoso
hand

If anything was ever done tell me?
one part the plane his mouth opened

gasping Lenny's biography slowly I
trembled vibratory she must make
verses behind the dissection traced
his ancient palms

mistrusts little Leo na r do
a certain Caterina sniffed an art
historian probably a peasant girl

my love gallops sang Flora benignly
now her face is smeared and powdered
my patch of scalp in the light
analyzed how the shroud was made

having all the facts of the young wife
exactly

expert chipping inward opened rows
into space red see Mona between
the livid

cyclic flow worries Sigmund trembled
in those things which appeared
wonderful to others

a round-buttocked young nude male
deepening the suture crooned Lenny

drawing the musculature screwed
a lira here a lira there slowly my
sweetness I bent backwards my spine
where the ribs arise

which end in the neck and raise up
the face is smeared and powdered

which end in the neck and depths
numbered simultaneously mistrusts
Flora a certain Caterina sniffed an
art historian probably a peasant girl

into the verbal portrait and as light
of candle and night and paper on which
you were writing were beginning

the drawings breaking through mortar

and as the light of the candle seg-
mented the testicle

I played with a conscious and virtuoso
hand

my slow molecular orgasm recycles
Lenny's dark sayings

cut two replace the precise
curvature whorls sperm sweat vocaboli
mundane jottings

pepper century end slowly I paid
a heavy debt

dismiss me as a clever craftswoman
stagnates codifications pulsate
slowly the throat bursts floral
filled three felt the vomit

I should not jump the gun number
the drawings breaking through deviate
walls & mortar hexagons

and as the light of the candle
and the night and the paper on which
I was writing were coming to an end

wet blue mingled left to right diagrams
of a child of two years the name
of Mona back I traced her palms
illuminated crooned Sigmund layered
buds nailed your darkened uterus

floating into space

it seems that she always trembled
when she began to paint

a lira here a lira there slowly my
sweetness sighed Lenny coldly artful

I had to do it like this so that
the birds could sing

sketches cuts musculature segmenting
the invisible

fall to desire light weight when
darkened Lenny saw smeared the lup-
pud structuring felt the portrait
despoiled

I was so easy a death intoned Flora
squeezed between flames there a
trembling paysanne takes apart

end wet blue mingled right to left
sinuous flayed diagrams a child of
two years in which she found everything
to be opposite

I turned to your side posed brush

that sketch kneeling with data raw
complexity and if you can draw me
Mona could not put three persons
still halved moist fitted stubborn

one folds his tunic freshly but then
the boy's abdomen tensed fragmentary
blue design white in cloth sucked
flame light & heat fat network

designed arteries folded her tunic
'neath her head made vibratory

And I traced the palms forces darkened

before me only collapse of ground-back
figures half her own name   tell me if
anything was ever done make the drawing
lactarious

brush encase the lup-pud even
the masterwhole even scratch
Lenny's palms obsessive his

mouth opened repeating a lira
here a lira there vocaboli sweat
sperm saturated the canvas shape
of a peasant girl weeping your
pale & gasping Sigmund mistrusts
felt colored dots behind

the dissection left mingled wet
inflated the testicle coldly artful
so that when Flora painted spirals
left to right mingled she drew

my long gray hands my throat

nailed into space I had superimposed
flayed the ground back Lenny's
biography intoned Mona a certain
Caterina sniffed an art historian

you could not put now her face is
smeared and powdered light the patch
analyzed your verses halved in cloth
lactarious

You turned to my side splinters
spaced across my dark sayings tricky
hand slit crossed

overflowing the atelier sucking
a cold solution splashing buds
layered walls & mortar & the night

as the light of the candle
sides expert comes to a halt
painting betrayed your pale

& gasping son continuous dissection
drops pressed veils the smirking
paysanne snipping her braid glued
your long gray hands she drew

the same drawing the two follicles
pointed Lenny's eyes hatching

America the cruel virgin rolling
crossed you are about to say
something about oil & bread rush
and the flowers

nailed into space the knotted braids
spouts of Flora's own hair motion

of the brat's vomit spreading sweetness
spiral in the water floral trembled
coldly artful details my dark sayings
weeping your pale & gasping Sigmund
licking wisdom shoulders squaring

angled into space recto spaces across
images Mona's future nailed into space
weight of soil sifted Leo na r do

began by noting exactly as the light
your pale & gasping Sigmund between
flames sleight of hand tricky

simpered Lenny you detected faults

the text slit erect I played with
a conscious and virtuoso hand

traced jottings segmenting
smeared lightly lightly smeared
Leo na r do alone double experience

rose like a column of blood 'neath
your shimmery hayre seams depths
loosened notebooks rose up   recto
linear only there & here step by
step Mona said Flora had caught
a chill searching dazed tell-tale
only for herself as light of candle

& night & paper on which I was
writing were coming to an end

Sigmund crooned Lenny whines at length
how much more difficult it is to
understand works of nature than book
of a poet

because her hands chose of their
own accord shaking demolishing
flayed diagrams so that my throat
saturated spirals rolling glued
your sleight of hand drawing hidden
pictographs

because your hands knotted
my dark sayings his itching scrotum

he always trembled when she began
to paint

a lira here a lira there paper
curvature sperm vocaboli

Find the name of Mona perforated
she was the architect scanning
viewing above her raised

dimension ovum spermatozoon
blood propelling down in painting
the portrait

you were the outlines origins
traced said poignant Lenny

because Flora's splashing a cold
solution across her biography details
Lenny's dark sayings

She was the germinal of travail
sculptor painter musician engineer
and scientist palms stroking
your patch of scalp repeating
a lira here a lira there

his breast itching your pale
& gasping Sigmund segmented across
the unknown contours of the atelier
slowly he paid a heavy debt

molecular activity hexagons of
pure & noble flows burnt the sun
would not have filtered a burnt
hidden caricature

of Lenny's lifetask triumph
details in Mona's fibers into
the verses

Pools

after they had left there   witness

a few years after the conquest
so that the Spaniards crossed recrossed

origin and emigrations the quest for
shining dawn
Spanish soaking cell by cell spreads over
gold sheets of gold leaf spirals

sunlight beaten into birds pumas jaguars

birds pumas jaguars serpents coil

so that the Spaniards seized the gold
faint cuts until you stare down close
you stare down close into heat widening
your nostrils smell the paste of corn

when the Spaniards invaded the land

the fields ancient corn plants rivers
ravines multiplying birds pumas jaguars
serpents nuggets flakes grains dust

dust of Aztec names Moctezuma where
they built temples witness

walls of a circular house raw thongs
raw thongs hanging strips of blanket
woven into birds pumas jaguars

birds pumas jaguars serpents coil

smoke behind from a sixteenth of one
burns paint Salia measures light then
traces his forearm tightens

you calculate every inch then take
between your

between your long gray hands resin
cast lots with a handful of corn
spilling

every inch lactarious you mistrust
holes in the hands and feet Sigmund
gently taps his finger
marks time backwards points at walls

a circular house saw raw thongs
bloody widening holes

tied your neck and feet together

hanging upon a cross you stare down
see pools of black paint glistening
then an old Osage woman stretched
upon a cross

black paint blisters in the sun
circles of skin nearer and nearer
she looked at a photograph

her saliva pools behind her teeth
when gravel sand blown on wind

wiped out these lines on a chart bringing
our wonder two hundred Spaniards saw land
spread over with stones under the weight
that night sunk each part

each part more molecular that red earth

you heard their voices ordering us to brand

human figures the skin opening shone reddish-
yellow mistrust imprints of hardened letters
you are reading about the quest for gold

each part that she feels the skin of the drum
you said to us keep on diagonal methodical
burned your desire and delight of letters

burns yellow skin half salt that water
from drum drunk spreads over deep pink
punctures you heard their voices

their voices ordering us to brand
we remind you of grass pushing through opening
through opening cracks

as a stream of molten lava spreads over
that island a cold molecular fire
I order you to fill in dark ridged slowly
three wounds one in the thigh one in the head

one in her left arm red dots grow into holes

her attention spans species of plants floating
a warm dry wind that blows for days

Black Chalk

cleaved olive pits hidden in Salia's
muscle ligament she began working
right to left while Flora was

seeding wild corn

bent down tested with her tongue
blood blood and light silent see
Lenny trampling a serpent fixed palest
patina molten only color rubbed seeding

lilies daisies dahlias

A paysanne exposed faults sketched
a sac of blood then you turned leaves
here there like props looking for actors

ransacked cunningly Flora's labor
done in chalk and pen tell-tale Salia
Flora smooths black chalk cast chalk
back calculating ribbons of cartilage

in chalk and pen now show him apples
yellow skin a headless idol work of

a headless idol work of another
anonymous master tell-tale gouged skulls
cold yellow

in winter then I came across earthworms

Leo na r do's eyes deep pink stare
upwards downwards moved over half-silvered
muscle ligament

your gracile brow-ridge faults sketched
she was drawing clots segments blue
spattered right to left washed against
dissections

you saw Lenny bending over Salia
tested with his tongue wondrously
because as every inch fills cleaved veins
whispered Salia now just show my blood
and light

now just show my blood and light silent

see me trampling a serpent
then she came across piles of gouged skulls

filled with molten bronze

cleaved olive pits hidden in Salia's remnants

in terracotta or marble they began working
lilies dahlias daisies that apples
in hands of Flora

wild fruits & nuts

lilies daisies dahlias when
when you turned your head in that direction
wrought variations rotating

knots necks heads apertures   A column
giving way heaved up the soil splits
surgical scar stains terracotta marble
half-twisted veins plants fissures

cleaved olive pits hidden in Salia's hidden
pits hidden in Salia's remnants Sigmund
reflected

then you came across piles of gouged skulls
filled with molten bronze

kneeling he smooths black chalk
now show my eyes looking at that idol
tell me when you came upon him
Bloody she came forth stepping forwards
cleaved Salia's sections

when Lenny judges her now show her
now show her displaying her version
now destroy his version

tell me who assures you that
this work ever was

hair and water locked molecular
Digging with trowels black chalk and ash

when Leo na r do inked over with
naked eye then he came across hair

across hair and water when she came
upon him bloodstained trampling a serpent
kneeling Flora's hard muscle burnished
wood

then he came across gouged skulls
lip-synced Sigmund filled with molten
with molten bronze

Lenny needs a fine awl to pierce parchment
stitching points gold & blue heads
mistrusts Mona that this work ever
tightening

gut thread through which water water
runs out of his side

Mona's faults sketched composed heavy
filled with molten bronze
when you judge her now show her now show
her displaying my version

cut carefully veins plants deception
then you came across piles of gouged
across piles of gouged skulls

filled with molten bronze

Flora stepped backwards
cast the head sphere   It seems I had

isolated windpipe she was folding
the fallen figure right to left

he inked over my version working
gut thread through which water water
runs out of his side

chalked out veins plants Lenny's
faults never tiring of deception

her muscle ligament cold yellow
in chalk and pen traces
diagrams erupting beneath stone pulls
the jaw from the skull spots
spots damaged segments she inked over
his version tightening her fingers

removing smudged diagrams with naked
eye then she took a fine awl to pierce
parchment threading muscle ligament
left to right porous

nearly imperceptible

Flora's hair bloodstained then she
came across image of a seated woman

her gracile brow-ridge faults sketched
her own bones flared cartilage
wrapped fragments hidden

itself light color only skeleton pulls
the jaw why did your face just now
now show me skeletons and corpses

Flora whisked cold ash piles sand pulls
the jaw from the skull half-kneeling stares
at Salia's sections gracile brow

lilies daisies dahlias
that apples in hands of Flora yellow
in winter then she came across earthworms
Leo na r do's eyes deep pink

now just your blood and light silent
now show me mastoid process before her
broken apples one hidden in the smock
hidden in the smock of Salia
in the smock hidden fragments

Swollen rubbed seeding half-tested with
his tongue work of anonymous master

broken into black chalk faults layers
ribbons of cartilage olive pits cleaved
Salia's sections remnants

cleaved Salia's sections just blood just
blood and light lilies daisies dahlias
mused Sigmund

ash and blood wedged in the portrait
segments of stalks sprouting
red wild corn succored

ash layered across work of another
anonymous master and light blinking
against white plaster cleaved Salia's

white plaster cleaved Salia's sections
bloodstained charred by fire pulled
bodies axis Flora drops yellow apples
whispered Sigmund tell my version

work of another anonymous master

sand piles pulls skeleton Flora feels
twisting fibers her alluring diagrams
Sigmund mused brushing a fly from
his notebook one leaf turned

whoever looks at that idol
red wild corn succored
it is Leo na r do eating bread and
drinking wine traces of fish oil
he smoothed his rouged lips blood

smoothed his rouged lips blood and light
lip-synced Sigmund

cloth stained with herbs and vegetables
Lenny had gouged circles painting
gouged circles painting fissures
stained glass deep pink bread and wine

Flora soaking cloth in elder flower

this circle of blood now tell-tale
Salia twisting under the smock

as Flora smooths black chalk half-
kneeling when your eyes cast back-and-
forth the fallen figure cast back
demoniacal he tested with his tongue

blood and light lip-synced Sigmund
isolated now why did Leo na r do
mused Salia hair and water fixed
palest patina molten

because as every inch across left to
right whoever looks at that idol
when her eyes cast cold yellow isolated
ribbons of cartilage windpipe olive pits
swathed Salia's sections in elder flower

tell me who assures you that this
that this work ever was

then you came across piles of gouged
skulls Flora said now show me layering
blue linen lilies dahlias daisies

Salia's sections remnants acidifying
done in chalk and pen now show me apples
white skin a headless idol

work of another anonymous master

after painting all your life quickly

Leo na r do smoothed yellow clay
soaking brushes his smock counting
circles shifted his weight stepped
backwards drinking wine

isolated now why did she swath Salia's
she swathed Salia's sections
doubled over measures

Flora measures a headless idol palest
a headless idol palest patina molten
because as every inch across left
left to right

that night Mona mixing blood and ash

all soil was once rock broken porous
once rock broken porous splits
tell-tale as we whispered

Lenny watched Mona measuring pilasters
a lira here a lira there
work done in chalk and pen back-and-
forth he stepped backwards mistrusts

faults mistrusts
one for the squirrel one
now Salia half-kneeling cast

cast blood and light light blinking
against white plaster Flora whispered

Leo na r do stepped backwards calculated
muscle in gold and silver isolated windpipe
he was drawing blue segments

never tiring of deception vivifying
cut tomato vines sketched faults
how drops of paint hair and water heaved
when you sponged

your neck to the side shape of a peasant
girl twisting under the smock spattered

menstrual lup-pud Flora's muscles harden
drawing brushed

all the senses lactarious pia mater
dura mater she was drawing opening wounds
grinding cracks and chips shape devoured

opening wounds shape of cracks stained
glass inserted half-twisted

spirals earthworms because as every inch
fuels conjures mused Sigmund his neck
to the side riddled tears drawings
of a child before you added Flora

Lenny voyages all over Venice Pisa

across skull of a child

white skin a headless idol

Flora's hand drawing hair and water
now show Lenny counting

a lira here a lira there
piles sand green sheep manure
disposed soaked herbs and vegetables

you watched Mona measuring pilasters
Mona measuring pilasters now show her
now show her long gray hands

mixed blood and ash

tomato vines a sac of blood pulled right
to left from bogs absorbed fluids
from walls running into roots

from rows of shadowed apertures
sighed Sigmund

tell me who assures you that
this work ever was

gravel sand clay silt freezing
mixed blood and light
then you came across earthworms

all soil was once rock loosened
your smock

your neck to the side angled reading
this tale mistrusts

all soil was once rock
kneeling Flora's hard muscle
Flora's hard muscle burnished wood

bathing she saw Lenny preparing
diligently mused Sigmund
flowers and crops phosphorus

tell me when you came upon her
trampling a serpent now show him
searching faults now just sand piles
mistrusts Flora that this rock
yellow sand Flora looking at scalp
daisies

splitting that dim dark corner

when you used shade like props
faced her painting my outlines

the tree stood in water
near yellow remnants as white boughs
forced down the soil
left to right pulled by skill & art

etching the beautiful face of Salia

it is Mona eating bread and drinking
wine traces Flora's hard muscle
burnished wood

work of another anonymous master

rapidly rare flowering traces image
of a paysanne Mona now with chalk
now Mona with chalk and pen sketched
with pen and chalk her neck shadowed

segments her version smudged Lenny's
version

it is Leo na r do eating bread and
drinking wine traces fish oil slowly
water drains through sand blinking light

particles nearly imperceptible
Flora fingers yellow clay shaping
muscle ligament your gaze mused Sigmund

when I judge her labor now show her half
in light and shadow on a scaffold painting
measuring pilasters

broken porous splits

You have turned your head slowly searching

your scalp sutured exposed
joints veins paint spirals   but Mona
suffered while binding Salia's sections

I the young cornstalk

his fingernails only light
nearly imperceptible

veins filled tightening

your gracile brow-ridge Lenny needs
Lenny needs a fine awl to pierce
parchment examines gut thread mistrusts
you turned your head

Bloody he came forth her eyes deep pink
stare kneeling she examines fissures
her neck angled lip-synced Sigmund mistrusts
now in hands of Flora

lilies dahlias daisies
then she took hidden fragments

her fingers traced faults across mistrusts
image of a seated woman

Mona said like props looking for actors

It seems I heard Leo na r do saying
your face which once I wept for dead

clots Lenny's speech whispered Salia
she smoothed yellow clay hard   Beware
contriver Sigmund mused

gravel sand clay silt blown on wind
as white forced down forwards
silt blown on a scaffold

crevice in rock silt frost soon porous
flesh

like props looking for actors I designed
a sac of blood manic smiled Lenny your
first portrait pulsates as every inch
measured when you used shade like

like props looking for actors
doses of nitrogen and copied a sac
of blood half-kneeling she analyzed
how drops of paint hair and water

outlines of a serpent mused Sigmund
his neck angled mistrusts
I have sutured work of another twisted

tomato vines muscle ligament flowering

piles sand green sheep manure yellow
manure yellow forced down as white
forced down as white boughs splitting
lines fluid

your fraudulent process conjures
pia mater dura mater

Mona said I watched a fallen log
a fallen log sinking when gravel sand
clay silt blown on wind

accumulate under the canvas frost
mistrusts added dimension texture
first the portrait

where a sac of blood reflects

blood reflects and the night air
bayberry rosa rugosa blossom Sigmund
touched his tongue your neck angled
smiled your rouged lips

drained twisted tomato vines muscle
your forearm mistrusts sand clay silt
blown pulsates Mona calculates conjures
pia mater dura mater

where a sac of blood reflects loosened

loosened her braids counting particles

milkweed crust ash while Salia eating
Salia eating bread and drinking wine
smiled Lenny when his head lowers
measured

when you designed a sac of blood manic
your fingernails like props looking
like props looking for actors shade

doses of nitrogen your head angled
mistrusts now show her brushing
shadowed on the walls
Tlaloc

on one knee she sketched corbels dug
her fingernails shaping rotates

to the bare bones Sigmund dreamed
all in black my love watered around
watered around roots drained clay
when gravel pulsates

image of a seated woman silt then
you took hidden

that air around pulled cloth blown

blown on wind parchment breathes
exposes skull scalp small muscles
there a paysanne on one knee sketched
those things that appeared

those things that appeared wonderful
there she assembled the first portrait
Flora right-handed flinging kernels

I'm a hungry bum searching the seams
of a discarded wallet

that air around routes now forced jets
now forced jets blood through silt
your neck white-edged light blues
junipers

on one knee he sketched leaves

sketched white wings

shadowed on the walls now forced
his forearm faults in gold and silver

Seeds of Fire

rotates shaping Flora's hard muscle
slow chalk lilies dahlias daisies
small muscles white-edged each day
etching

etching seeds of fire

now a cold wind that dim dark corner
splitting Flora analyzes she sketched
corbels dug her fingernails

all in black my love Sigmund mused

on one knee Flora examined loosened
loosened her braids searching routes
white-edged her neck angles right
to left her saliva accumulates

your head lowers repeating her version
splits porous image drained clay when

when gravel pulsates Leo na r do
examined his fingernails his head
his head angled mistrusts now show

now show him shadowed on the walls

smegma reflects drinking wine
you watched a fallen log sinking

etching seeds of fire lip-synced Sigmund
now a cold wind gravel sand my image

my image of a paysanne on one knee

quickly your painting
skin color worked that night mixing blood
and ash pen and ink filling
night mixing blood

before you broken pilasters cornice corbels

now forced his forearm lowers coldly faults
sand gravel now forced jets of ink
this work exposed demoniacal spread grimly
cloth pulled my long gray hands

cut carefully veins plants deception
you watch Lenny with the same smock

isolated wearing a surgical mask
his forearm pulsates lowers calculates
my fallen figure intoned Sigmund

Beware contriver Flora saw Mona working
in gold and silver shadowed sections
shadowed in white flames

that air around roots soil clay drained
rot milky angled her neck to the side
her windpipe seamed shadowed on the walls
drawing leaves and roots inserted
Aztec names Tlaloc
leaves and roots inserted a particle

pulled filled every inch routes when gravel
routes when gravel sand clay silt blown
sand clay silt blown on wind

I watched a fallen log sinking

Salia's saliva measured while Leo na r do
breathes

air shadowed leaves only her fingernails
porous blazed downwards while shaping hair
hair and water weight reverses searching
then I took hidden fragments

measuring muscle ligament now a cold wind
now a cold wind piles sand your fingernails
sketched gravel sand as white boughs

my fingernails sketched tell-tale measured
Salia's saliva

Leo na r do drops on one knee mused Sigmund

half-kneeling in soil then angles reverses
his weight sketched tomato vines muscle
ligament now a cold wind

now a cold wind splits hard yellow hard
yellow a cold wind in light in light

in light and shadow

sweetens leaves exposes hidden fragments
Flora rinses them in water and copied a
sac of blood half-kneeling she analyzes
how drops of hair paint and water
clay silt blown on wind doses of nitrogen
mistrusts

image of a seated woman now she pierces
parchment examines gut thread

how sand clay silt blown on wind when
drawing his flesh your forearm your
forearm pulsates
flesh your forearm lowers

your forearm coldly artful
Flora's hard muscle burnished wood

Lenny calculates how gravel sand clay
now show her loosened braids brushing
her notebook when she judges when
her head lowers

repeating her version Lenny watched
her labor rapidly rare flowering traces

image of a paysanne eating bread and
drinking wine traces fish oil slowly

fissures in clay rock faults spirals
she smoothed her rouged lips whoever
looks at that idol when gravel sand

when gravel sand clay silt blown on wind
chalk nearly imperceptible
splits porous broken counting

I watched a fallen log sinking
his fingernails searching a particle
angles his neck he was drawing

blood sketched when you judge his

when you judge his version his long
slow fingers twisted tomato vines muscle
crevice measured Salia whispers stares
kneeling on one knee

Beware contriver sketched tell-tale
tell-tale across how drops of blood
saturate around roots
I the young cornstalk

blazes down loosened milkweed crust ash
soil grass animal outlines of a serpent
pulsate you examined diagrams measured

your head lowers exposes skull scalp
exposes skull scalp parchment

and the night air reflects gravel sand
clay silt now in hands of Mona lilies
in hands of Mona lilies she smoothed
yellow clay

It seems I heard a fallen log sinking
shadowed on the walls

slowly I mesmerize Lenny's speech clots

biography blood fir palms
then you took exposed
you took exposed milkweed crust ash
your fraudulent process Sigmund reflects

water held there her fingernails
sketched tell-tale across

across a headless idol when gravel sand
clay silt blown on wind

sinking a fallen log I watched
Leo na r do kneeling isolated never
never tired of deception

etching the beautiful face
she stepped backwards smooths black
chalk loosened her braids her long
slow counting
one for the squirrel one for the crow

counting broken porous splits
drains rapidly through light
through silt blown on a scaffold

Leo na r do's fingers trace slowly
his version searching left to right
Flora's hard muscle burnished
muscle burnished wood

Leo na r do sections gravel sand clay
mistrusts

when you judge her labor now show
now show her half in light and shadow
her neck angled she was drawing
lilies dahlias daisies

then Salia sprinkling as leaves sweeten
when soil becomes magical Sigmund said
supple animal outlines you looked at
her forearm tendons

then watched pulsations fissures
pulsations fissures heard sand gravel
tossed by Salia blowing up a pig's bladder

Flora washing clay silt as autumn winter
clay silt as autumn winter curling space

inhales Salia's breath as soil around roots

and sweetens leaves as autumn winter
Flora was drawing lilies dahlias
she looked upward saw Salia's impudent
mouth blowing up a pig's bladder

her outlines light purple as autumn winter
disgorges ash crust plant sinking ash crust

sinking through silt then Lenny saying
Lenny saying your fraudulent process
rouging his nipples deep pink

Salia seated on a scaffold watched from above
took delicate blossoms pierced milkweed crust

disgorges dark greens she began working

dark greens he began working cell by cell
dug silt then Mona took delicate blossoms
like props looking turns her head

quickly skin and night leaves near
you saw how Salia drawing a plow oxen
plowing and sowing

I watched a fallen log sinking

Mona loosened her fingers your green
fingers your green thumb Sigmund repeats
so what do you do if you do not dig
near a pile of broken pilasters filled
his pockets clay sand

sketched gravel sand skull scalp
skull scalp parchment float in air

skull scalp parchment opening ground
pulsates image edges of Mona's smock
dark green seamed

flesh your forearm angled muscles yellow

muscles yellow float in air

her slow molecular orgasm

the figure's upper torso splits detours
as autumn winter now show Salia
now show Salia rouging his nipples
then traces pulsations light purple

through which water runs out of her
water runs out of her side
stared down wearing a surgical mask

digging locked this now show
now show my eyes looking at that idol
clinging humus

black chalk and ash filled then I
came forth stepping forwards spread
paint thickly idling but

as leaves lit this hole from the wound
your pale & gasping son you seated yourself
rouging his lobes my saliva glistening
her inlines pulsate edge swerve

slowly she rouges her nipples

clay sand gravel
her saliva pools behind his teeth
planting still loosens clutches bones
disgorge
I the young cornstalk
rose like a column of blood

plowing and sowing
splits terracotta marble cleaved olive
cleaved olive pits Salia idling but
drawing a plow oxen plowing
and sowing

Flora rotates her wrist her forearm
tendons Salia loosened her fingers
took delicate blossoms clinging

clinging humus
Flora smiled braiding her hair
shaping each autumn winter lowers

depth blocked full nightfall between
end of Flora's labor whoever draws her
playing like a child fingers shadowed
Salia's hands milky with light

I felt my brow weighed down by splendor
chanted Flora

until desire to draw pulsations your
forearm lowers circles on wind frost
between nightfall

Leo na r do never tired of deception
shadowed on the walls edges of his
edges of his outlines

I watched a fallen log sinking disgorges
outlines then she tossed delicate
she tossed delicate blossoms loosened
slowly sand gravel

twisting outlines her palms chalky
she smoothed yellow clay glowing
nearly imperceptible tell-tale
Sigmund watched Lenny

between nightfall filling his pockets
filling his pockets soil grass skulls
disgorged

idol when gravel sand blown on wind

FLORA'S LABOR

struck their faces then remnants of
a cold molecular cloud slowly sand gravel

shaping tendons then she came forth
she came forth dancing disgorged
the ants stealing flowers twisting between
nightfall

Flora sketched skulls grass crevice clumps
head of a mushroom show her menacing
the ants as autumn winter burns veins

burns veins in rock spirals dug each
idol rose nearly as high as the scaffold
Salia idling but drawing a plow

oxen plowing and sowing

lowers his head sinking a paint brush
creating black ants from the paste
from the paste of the corn

I the young cornstalk rose like a

column of blood

she turns her head now she examines
surgical strokes casts off a thousand
cleaved olive pits Flora's labor clouds

twisting outlines then filled clinging
humus disgorges inlines now she
examines Aztec names Tlaloc

I heard crows their claws searching

on a scaffold stare while Flora after
washing clay silt measured veins in rock
her gracile brow she designed forced

forced image it seems I heard Leo na r do
saying your fraudulent process his fingernails
black dug in gravel deep pink crust ash
roots exposed crevice Salia seated

on a scaffold watched from above rotates
his ankle then the brat took delicate blossoms

rocked in Flora's arms loosened her braids
smiled Lenny's rouged nipples burning
pierced milkweed crust manic his fingernails
like props looking like props looking

brushing her hair Mona smiled her neck
Mona smiled her neck white-edged Sigmund
conceived his face to the bare bones

cleaved as wax of candle breathed small
muscles fissures her image of a paysanne
a paysanne turns her head now she examines
Aztec names Tlaloc
turns her head rotates her ankle shaping
clay her forearm white-edged she will fix
white-edged she will fix one segment
parchment Flora's work her notebooks

her notebooks just of drawings appeared
wonderful Lenny said before he breathed
half-kneeling

plant as autumn winter curling space
atmosphere dark burning Leo na r do's

Leo na r do's design sweetens turns Salia's
skull of a child coated his fingernails
sand clay silt blown right to left rosa
bayberry blossom

then it comes from bones white-edged
etching first light purple until beautiful
peaks depths measured silt he will

he will fix one segment his head turns
towards Salia seated on a scaffold Salia

eating bread now show him shadowed
now show him shadowed on the walls

splitting roots wearing a surgical mask
quickly your painting air leaves white
air sand gravel when Salia turns right
to left counting splits clay

rosa bayberry blossom in hands of Salia
you smoothed yellow clay when you judge
diagrams counting slow broken
as autumn winter

ash crust deep pink roots pierced
angles her neck she was drawing
animal outlines of a serpent Salia's
fingers trace slowly

slowly my fingers plant now show
now show yourself kneeling searching
left to right diagrams muscle rapidly

rapidly through light sand clay silt
smoothed bayberry air leaves her
swallowing water

Salia seated on a scaffold   And you looked
upward saw Salia's impudent face crying

Salia's face
dreamed white-edged his face to my fingers
pierced milkweed crust manic   She sought
peace washing clay silt measured veins
fissures Flora's design

roses growing in concrete deep pink rot
depths plant as autumn infinitely built
up lines through which water

through which water runs out of her side
echoes Leo na r do pierced milkweed crust
counting slow all the delicate blossoms

and sweetens leaves as autumn winter
now show Mona her neck angled she was
neck angled she was drawing lilies dahlias
wearing a surgical mask

splitting roots show now my labor
I began to paint

ice left behind sun blazes down
slant of the wall

wax of candles dark green
dark green on the wall of the atelier
sculptural depth

each autumn winter   blanket ash crust
leaves dust grains now Flora salvages
herbs lowers her wrist draws water

fog winds blizzards shrivel rot leaves
pots filled with light soil crumbles apart
rotate purple traces clay rock
Salia climbing on a scaffold

he heard crows their claws searching

isolate one third of the portrait's seams

it seems she heard crows their claws
their claws searching Sigmund intoned
she began with her little drawings
exploits

Tell me who assures you that this
work ever was

water salt sugar protein
smoke of a fired kiln bright-red coals
wrought coldly artful
brushing Lenny's beard reverses your

pale & gasping son

rouging his nipples Leo na r do

you must slowly outline a serpent
a serpent coated deep pink segment
ash crust plant skull then tracing
Mona yellow as leaves sweeten

as leaves sweeten blossom Flora counts
as autumn winter disgorges dark greens
you began working cell by cell

sweetens segments inserts faults
cords through layers

tell me who assures you that this work
that this work ever was

pierced roots gracile brow sand clay
silt burning right to left dormant
shape blood jets through silt I heard
a fallen log sinking a headless idol

splits blankets ash crust plant skull
as autumn winter now show Flora
drawing animal outlines of a serpent
when Salia climbing on a scaffold
stared down wearing a surgical mask

then traces pulsations light purple
Flora and Mona watched tell-tale
Sigmund lip-synced

suffer the cells in the evening light

below all brushed your blanket
sutured

one for the cutworm one for the crow

hinged space festering

you looked upwards saw a pig's bladder
in the heat of the sun filling
disgorged in darkness plastic tubes
glistening lip-synced Sigmund

stared down wearing a surgical mask
sutured plague tribes crossed
pierced my flesh

horse and rider whispered Sigmund
I the young cornstalk mixed with
segments flames brushing

disgorged skull neck reddish eyes
reddish eyes of the serpent

in the evening light tribes crossed
outlines twisted deep pink plague

counting one for the cutworm
one for the crow

unhinged its jaw extracting a single
tooth

she heard crows their claws searching

Mona calculates gravel sand clay silt
blown on wind

trees in autumn winter pulsate vines
vines isolate Mona guessed then sketched
bright-red stems counting dark greens
dark your outlines

as he looked upward saw Salia's impudent
mouth blowing up a pig's bladder
now winter autumn ash crust deep pink

rouging his nipples   Salia stares down
from a scaffold inhales lilies dahlias
daisies loosens his smock
a paysanne crumbles herbs her fingernails
drawing leaves

doses of nitrogen muscle saliva of Salia
paint water hidden image splits
now in hands of Flora yellow clay
she washes clay disgorges

ash crust Lenny began working cell
began working cell by cell

Mona's dark green smock unwinding

pulsates edges near a pile of broken
near a pile of broken pilasters

formed remnants fainter when water

when water weakened the walls of
the atelier Mona drew together

drew together the current and spaced
ancient corn plants

of yellow corn and of white corn
Flora made their flesh mixed with
mixed with the blood of the serpent

you lower your wrist arching your
glowing palm slowly kernels reveal
veins pulsating

I heard crows their claws searching

swerving towards Tenochtitlan routes
to the pupil of Mona's left reddish
Mona's left reddish eye searching

Tenochtitlan

still Lenny's hands milky with light
flickered coated bone flakes

horse and rider around the fire
mused Sigmund engulfed by the serpent

silence and slow soaking

heaved up the soil waves flow over
waves flow over blood fir biography

still flowing   as ice   covered   ritual
planting Salia shovels gravel sand clay
clutches bright-red stems   as she

as she loosens her braids unwinding
manic her fingers expose disgorge
bones tendons & muscles waves rose

rose like a column of blood   splashes
pulse groups bathed fragments digging
fragments flesh biography blood fir
palms crush pigment then

Leo na r do's feast day began traced
crows their claws dark-green trees
pulsate ash crust crevice   she gouged
clay

behind ice   quickly he will fill canvas
image of a paysanne

gracile her brow unwinding her smock
slowly he rouges his nipples

deep pink crust ash autumn winter
rocks in Salia's hands moonlit vines
his saliva pools behind his teeth

ebb & flow then as we looked upward
saw Salia's impudent mouth dark rose
murmured into Lenny's ear Luca Luca

he stares down from a scaffold
half-kneeling your pale & gasping
your pale & gasping son

arches his back exposed there light
rose and the canvas on which
she was painting faults circular

deranged by skill & art each beginning
traces diagonal lines tribes crossed
under the trees recrossed

I'm a hungry bum searching the seams
of a discarded wallet

on horseback with their guns pursing
your lips mistrusts the assemblage
a swelling of the eye-lids eruptions
porous exposed a new country

splashes black urine stained windows
of a cathedral multiplying his fingers
widening recrossing nerves

two halves there a scalp sutured

beating drum and whistle

stretching and dressing the skins
Mona purses her lips measuring faults

wounds her palms jagged sketches
cleaved Salia's sections
your whitish bones plagued by doubt

scattered   cremains

DRUM AND WHISTLE

into the vast heat of spirals because
your whitish bones

beating drum and whistle
morning sun multiplying her fingers

loosened her braids her long slow

searching encased skull neck body
skull neck body around roots yellow skin
floating like props looking

I heard crows their claws searching

their veins and tendons scattered
as leaves sweeten clay silt ash
your long gray hands cutting

measuring skull scalp parchment

her forearm tightens spreads over
blankets infected with plague seeding
spirals of heat loosens her braids

black urine runs through silt ash clay
shadowed on the walls spilling
walls spilling sand and gravel

a lira here a lira there

sutured through her ruptured flesh

tightens cords in Leo na r do's fingers
elbow shoulder hip
And in heel of cadaver smoke invades

one for squirrel one for crow

And if you shake leaves feverish master
skin paint surgical scar riddled
bright-red stems freezing paint

freezing urine blood segmented cell
segmented cell by cell prototypes
saturated he then looked at a circular

looked at a circular house walls
sand gravel beating drum and whistle
deep pink plague as autumn winter
rubs black clay

silence walls in remorseless then
she looked at a circular house
when you looked your veins multiplying
splashes black urine

they stare down on horseback pursing
their lips measuring ransacking
fingers crusted fibrous entrails

invades cadaver aluminum walls in

your neck to side

you read parts of the manuscript wrong
suppose

she reveals peculiar forms
them vivifying cording everyday
ash and blood whole aluminum pits

groups of the first Spaniards in America

On a second voyage to Tenochtitlan
moves hydrogen helium

Lenny's blanket wrapped around parts
of the dissection suppose red wild corn
smoke from a burning log

the wiry brat ejaculates
every foot-print of Flora multiplying
your long gray hands stretched your

gray hands stretched deer skin

Mona made rings gloves crowns masks
the outlines of a new country

Leo na r do seized the wrist of
the brat squeezed his throat blood
behind his teeth

placed the infected blankets one by one
stomach and bones crusted
for here leave sign of our fate

then he looked at a circular house

an old Osage woman crushing seeds
her iron-gray braids she gouged clay
quickly she pulls from fire

her saliva pools behind her teeth
she pulls from fire a pot spilling
morsels of beef half-kneeling Salia's
mouth measures walls

then quickly he will fill canvas
image of a paysanne flinging
a paysanne flinging kernels

unwinding her smock crows their claws
dark-green stained windows of a
stained windows of a cathedral

exposed a new country lip-synced Sigmund

you wrap a blanket around your waist
folds and gathers cross and recross

stakes with forked ends into ground
deep pink crust ash spirals of heat
I arch my back stretching it is
a paysanne bending

gracile her brow diagonal lines
skull neck you traced a scaffold
a forked tree

and close upon one of the horses
tendons & muscles glowing I saw Salia
beating drum and whistle

your palms crushing seeds showing
lines cross recross circular pulse
groups moist soil of names Cihuacoatl
bloody wing Huitzilopochtli bloody claw

faults she gouged clay I murmured
into Lenny's ear

groups of the first Spaniards in America
written on the stomach and bones
fragment shovels gravel sand clay

my doubt remains widening circles
circles slowly Leo na r do fingers
he rouges his nipples the brat stares
down from a scaffold arches his back
stretches his neck

riders cutting out entrails their lips
intone pulsate behind ice walls gouged
with names crossed recrossed tribes
on horseback

winding her iron-gray braids quickly
she fills canvas stretching roots
disgorges ancient corn plants

extracting one light amber stone

idol when gravel sand blown on wind
walls in flames of stone divided
roots

a black rain fell then silence and slow
soaking crust ash flames swerving
deep pink plague a forked tree
slicing their flesh

resin sap sweetens moonlit vines

Sigmund mused fascinated the Lords of
Mictlan horse and rider in darkness

searching Tenochtitlan still plastic tubes
glistening stared down in the Aztec inferno
in the evening light worshiped sticks
worshiped sticks of fat pine

I made rings gloves crowns masks
riddled with decay digging out a stone
leaving a stone

one for the cutworm one for the crow

lips whisper counting blankets infected

counting blankets infected with plague

one by one

They planted four acres wandering
east to west

from center smoke concentrated stems
burnt leaf white hearts of incense
palms arched pierced bleed names

Cihuacoatl bloody aluminum faults behind
ice walls density of scalp crusted
bark a forked tree shadowed upside-
down stems of moonlit vines you
mused

resin sap as leaves sweeten clay moss
of Florida through which blood jets

behind their teeth saliva red wild corn
multiplying ancient writing gouged in

gouged in the gourd seized a little man
Mona stares down following diagonal lines
surgical scar trusts her fibrous
skins dressing and stretching

measuring skull scalp parchment her
feast day

dark ridge of lava to north parched
halves of skulls placed one by one

one for the squirrel one for the crow

groups of the first Spaniards in America

they stare down on horseback

ride up close looking at fragments
slowly they circle you urge horse
and rider course toward in this
course toward in this direction tribes
crossed recrossed gouged signs

from armpit to stomach your pale
stomach your pale & gasping son loosens
his braids his throat pulsates saliva
pools behind his teeth scrotal sac
slit

groups of the first Spaniards in America

carcass stripped of its skin
bearing two halves there a scalp
two halves there a scalp sutured

crossed behind when they found ancient
corn plants she will find canvas
ash autumn winter discharging
pus from slit ears

your doubt remains for all that
you stretch your neck instinctively

Mona's attention drawn to reddish
layers glowing mudstone and sandstone
shovels gravel sand clay

clutches bright-red stems

tightens around roots woven veins
drew silence pale forests stretched
the canvas exposed ancient corn
plants shadowed upside-down

rifles against the walls
horse and rider around the fire

black urine soaking clay sand
as he loosens his braids fingers
dig

one for the squirrel one for the crow

crusted torn trees crash sounds
sounds of riders cleaning rifles

once Salia took an axe cut moonlit
vines saw bright-red surgical scar
through which blood

infected with plague the trunk
of the body engulfed by the serpent
two halves of the cadaver

slowly such great decay
Salia covered his head with Mona's
smock

child & Mona perched on Lenny's back

you stare down pursing your lips
your neck to the side
plagued by doubt

calculating strips of wood right
to left the weight of the corpse

one for the cutworm

and the night air blazes down her
jaw fused soil grass animal outlines
muscles slowly she reverses

one for the crow

changed nature of portrait strips
calculated left to right weight
of corpse one for cutworm down
her jaw slowly reverses cunningly

plagued by doubt his fallen figure
stained with blood of first person

ransacked cunningly you urinate
spontaneously while Flora flinging
while Flora flinging kernels

loosens her braids her smock unwinding
murmured into Salia's ear Luca Luca

I mesmerize intoned snake winding
covered their heads with blankets

black horns curve out sand mud
blue haze through woodland

a forked tree

you ride up close squeezing a staff
a staff with a skull splashes black urine

Mictlantecuhtli he who makes pus then hip shoulder
elbow and in heel of cadaver stomach
stomach and bones stretched out

he stares down on horseback pursing
their lips measuring strips of soil
strips soil riddled invades bright
bright red stems circles slowly

calculating strips walls in aluminum
analyzing death patterns blood segmented
cell by cell

deep pink plague slicing bright-red stems

their neck stretching left to right
their lips measuring ransacking

measuring ransacking entrails glistening
ash crust soaking
one for the cutworm one for the crow

dissected correctly counting plastic
plastic tubes filling

plastic tubes glowing in sunlight

you angled your face analyzing
death patterns

MULTIPLYING DEATH PATTERNS

one light amber stone red wild corn
dark ridge gouged

gouged configurations ripped two
halves two halves of parchment
multiplying death patterns

you put slashes in through which water
through which water runs spreads over
America through silt ash silt clay

death patterns plague crossed

I heard crows their claws searching

riddled bright red stems one gouged
exposed your whitish bones

exhausted outlines gravel sand skull
neck your wrists arch backwards crushing
backwards crushing seeds she wraps
a blanket through which blood

slowly such great decay
she stares down plagued by doubt

pus from slit ears horse and rider
in darkness tubes counted
one for squirrel one for crow

entrails walls freezing paint stained
circles on the stomach and bones

you ride up close begin searching
my painting two halves cut into side
deep pink crust heat from a burning log

internal and external burns glowing in sunlight
burns glowing in sunlight

widening a pair of jaws long slow
counting teeth burnt in fire
knife in one hand a blanket in the other
one hand a blanket in the other

gray hands stretched measured bones up close
ends cleaved deep pink marrow exposed
sections you analyze the assemblage

death patterns outlines of a new country

then Mona looked at a circular house
under the trees

she fasted scattered cremains
scattered cremains in the morning sun

ash blood black clay glowing in sunlight
death patterns floating like props
backwards one by one upside-down

image of a whipped and crucified woman
her saliva pools behind her teeth

then an old Osage woman crushing seeds
her palms shadowed Cihuacoatl bloody wing
Huitilopochtli bloody claw

notched stick end lower three long
strokes strokes from end to end

Flora waves her arm offering yellows
from plants from the stick towards
towards the sun her image crossed lines
paint congeals

you ride up close after each stroke
upper torso shadowed skull neck body

Salia details holes in the hands
and feet north of the fire peculiar
forms red stems splitting

Leo na r do makes a circular mark
passing his hands measuring skull scalp
parchment

Spaniards wearing braided silk belts
ropes used to pull the head and torso
elbows knees necks alternating

floating like props looking she heard

crows their claws searching

image of a whipped and crucified woman
her iron-gray braids hanging

end to end towards the sun following
crossed lines of paint lines cross
recross the center

freezing hard roots no sound no sound

of hoof-beats you ride up close
searching when you looked the heel
of the cadaver segmented cell by cell
encased roots

upper torso of the little man
multiplying seethed and probed
palms arch resin sap jets saturates
behind walls Salia's sketch of smoke

lines cross recross tendons veins
clutches bright red stems measuring
two halves of a circular house

sides of aluminum walls you stare down
on horseback you suppose she reveals
peculiar forms groups of

forms groups of the first Spaniards
in America

Leo na r do paints child & Mona as
leaves sweeten lip-synced Sigmund

Huitzilopochtli bloody claw Cihuacoatl bloody

bloody wing no sound no sound

scattered cremains in the morning sun
crossed lines of paint circles congeals
image of a whipped and crucified woman
her iron-gray braids hanging

BLACK STEMS

scattered cremains
through a woodland near a forked

near a forked tree patterns seeding
and yellow blossoms hydrogen green
You scattered delicate blossoms
my forearm tightens spreads over

right to left red stems counted one
for crow one for cutworm

the first skull showing lines crossed
recrossed yellow skin raw you stare
down into heat she falls backwards
mistrusts holes in the hands and feet

used nails every inch death patterns

circles spirals cross recross every
inch nearer and nearer into heat

his neck stretches Mictlantecuhtli he who
he who makes pus

every name shadows on the walls wind
spirals into heat spills sand gravel
you ride up close nearer and nearer

you use ropes to pull the head and torso

held her whitish bones high in air
near a forked tree broken rocks
a mile of black dust

whose names are gouged letters angled
white-edged your fingers through sand clay
through sand clay silt

your fingers tracing slant of wall
every inch mistrusts deviates

Tell me who assures you that this
work ever was

black stems sticking out letters planted
shape a headless idol crust ash then
you ride up close loosen your braids

hoof-beats swerving shadowed on walls
you heard crows their claws searching

black coals clumps of deep pink rot
fissures death patterns backflow crossed
left to right you are drawing raw thongs

image of a whipped and crucified woman
your saliva pools behind your teeth

you lower your wrist plagued by doubt
angled letters gouged into walls nearer
and nearer smoke from a burning cross

smoke from a burning cross spreads over
you looked at a photograph miles of
cracked clay walls of a circular house
spilling

blows sand on carcass near a forked tree
near a forked tree pointed tracks

broken rocks stained with blood
strips calculated weight and night air
measured outlines counted

counted one for crow one for cutworm

through woodland smoke from a burning
cross mistrusts you ride up close right
right to left of corpse staring down

analyzing death patterns jaw crushed
pus from slit ears deep pink marrow
deep pink marrow exposed

blue haze through woodland you heard
crows their claws searching
horses passing near a forked tree

hooves pointed tracks death patterns
bones black horns curve out sand mud
hooves crushing entrails bright red

bright red stems red wild corn slowly
ash crust soaking
Mictlantecuhtli he who makes pus you ride up
close stare down on horseback pursing

pursing your lips measuring claws
your neck stretches left to right nearer
and nearer

into heat yellow skin in sunlight
backwards smoke coils out of walls
walls of a circular house spilling

she rides up close raw thongs hanging
her veins and tendons nearer and nearer
spiral out backwards floating
took delicate blossoms one by one

held his whitish bones high in air
glowing in sunlight Cihuacoatl bloody wing
Huitzilopochtli bloody claw

begin searching photographs crossed
recrossed you stare down your neck
to the side plagued by doubt

what you will not find tightens circles
from a sixteenth of one
Salia's impudent mouth eating buttons

your forearm rubs ash showing lines
crossed recrossed reveals peculiar forms

smoke from a burning cross spirals
extracting one light amber stone idol
when gravel sand blown on wind

walls spilling she looked at a photograph
a circular house shadowed with names

every inch lactarious mistrusts

circles widening faint until her body

until her body hung wounded and bloody
gouged walls crust soaking
you light a match calculate weight of
carcass

her saliva pools behind her teeth
ash blood black paint covers
covers his teeth you ride up close
past death patterns

paint congeals internal and external
burns I ride up close stretches right
to left
near a forked tree backwards dragging
iron chains upper torso deep pink

suppose they make a circular mark
the hands and feet with lines cross
black stems glossy house paint

you mistrust holes in the hands
and feet he traces his palms
his palms in the darkness

then an old Osage woman stretched
stretched upon a cross tied with ropes
her iron-gray braids hanging

red stems protruding from black clay
burns in the wood

tightens ropes legs and hands shape
molds yellow skin marked patterns of

patterns of your iron-gray braids

then take between your long gray hands
resin cast lots with a handful of corn
blowing black dust green feathers

sunlight in every inch lactarious his
forearm rubs ash showing lines crossed
you mistrust a photograph circles gouged
dry black paint

the hands and feet pierced with holes

faint until her body nearer and nearer
the bone and cartilage the earth
slipping from a sixteenth of one

they ride up close there in a wood
near a forked tree crossed recrossed

tightens knots stretched upon a cross
hanging

ancient corn plants Flora's attention
tracks a circular mark when gravel sand
when gravel sand blown on wind

ice walls bleed names behind aluminum
ancient writing coils

along the edge he drew a circular mark
stripping bright red stems he mistrusts
faults dark ridged

gouged the corpse with a curved black
with a curved black horn

you feel as though you are plagued
by doubt counting
one cutworm one crow Mictlantecuhtli he who measures
ransacks

strips of blanket slowly such great decay

from his breast exhausted outlines
two halves of an amber stone

multiplying death patterns

while Flora flinging kernels right
to left inflames burns parchment
inserts ash crust soaking

soaking cell by cell spreads over
your whitish bones murmured into Salia's
mouth Luca Luca

intoned one for the crow one for
the cutworm you wrap a blanket around
your head eyes covered

deep pink plague nearer and nearer

how when the body of hair and water
vivifying

groups of the first Spaniards in America
under their clothing this triple-arm
cross their tongues pulsate

reciting oaths skulls and skeletons
discharging when water burns

when water burns tell us and instruct us
they feel two halves along the edge
the corpse gouged by a curved black
horn

blanket held your rigid fingers scattered
cremains she cuts a piece of parchment
exposes deep pink entrails he passes his

he passes his hands alternating ropes
used to pull the head and torso
cast lots with a handful of corn

molds shape the hard black stems

the death cart loaded with skulls
notched ends multiplying counted
the first skull they join searching

we light matches pegged joints
nearer and nearer into heat
inserting between ear and skull

ice nor the cold where they built
circular Flora divided two halves sides

sides of a house dry black paint
black paint along the edge exhausted
you have fallen

your attention passes to the holes
patterns mark her hands and feet

we mistrust the corpse gouged details
how the body of hair and water
now show yourself kneeling on gravel
counting Aztec names Tlaloc

between nightfall Flora draws her
iron-gray braids she passes near

near the death cart loaded loaded
with skulls ropes alternating
Leo na r do passes his hands he cuts
a piece of parchment his attention

tracks faults

he repaints the face hands background
cutting the parchment her wrist cramps
your forearm tightens circles of skin

blister between ear and skull

skull lacquered every inch you watch
segments scrape gravel sand there inches

there along the edge fields ancient
corn plants rivers ravines New Spain

naked scourgers stood in sunlight
He drinks in the holes in the hands

and feet he traces Tenochtitlan's terrain
seized raw thongs tightens knots

she takes upon her lap blankets strips
of blanket slowly wraps dark faults
molds shape of birds pumas jaguars

birds pumas jaguars serpents coil

faint until her body nearer and nearer
cuts your flesh Salia's impudent mouth
deep pink blows cremains he takes upon
his lap

a string of little skulls hides them

yellow smoke from a burning cross
Mona looks backwards at corner and sides
she makes a circular mark

she is drawing raw thongs letters gouged

Tell me who assures you that this work
ever was
she crosses left to right

then as she voyages lights a match

from a sixteenth of one hanging
legs and hands cartilage bone drawn
in black paint dust grains flakes

earth slipping ancient marks Utatlan
she looked at a photograph witness cell
by cell he stares down from walls

smells the paste of corn shapes loaves
of gold when the Spaniards invaded the land
witness there hanging strips when
the Spaniards fastened around their necks

hanging against white plaster walls

dead patterns she cuts corn plants
beats paste into thin sheets molds
shape she takes upon her lap

until your body nearer and nearer
segments

walls drawn in black paint you watch
clumps of black paint blister

clumps of black paint blister calculate
plagued by doubt when gravel sand
blown on wind gold dark ridged

cell by cell Spaniards track a circular
mark

A CIRCULAR HOUSE

dark faults their breasts and their

and their armpits opening I recognize
hydrochloric nitric acids Leo na r do smiles
you invoke the atmosphere display images
of penance she second only

only to a wooden statue her eyes covered
work of another anonymous master
he marks time backwards

so that the Spaniards seized the gold

they stare down close into heat
we smell the paste of corn water drains
through sand she drew the body

the body of hair and water deep pink
blowing black dust mounds in sunlight
lacquered skulls along the edge when
her skin lactarious

disgorges dark green routes then you
looked at a circular house

skin infected with plague your forearm
tightens ridges of hard silk slashes
days of the Aztec calendar cross expose
ancient corn plants

you mistrust lines of letters moving right
to left

cross platforms invoke infected

scraps of metal cartilage a string of
a string of little skulls tightly linked
use and reuse cell by cell Spaniards

drawn in black paint stare down from

stare down from white walls
you track ridged dark dead patterns

then birds pumas jaguars serpents coil
Sigmund reflects holes in the hands
in the hands and feet weight of the rifle
cuts your flesh you hoard gold sheets

of gold leaf spirals so that you seized
you seized the gold

between your long gray hands resin
cast lots with a handful of corn spilling

right to left you calculate every inch
dust of Aztec names Tlaloc where
a few years after the conquest

you stare down close see pools

see pools of black paint glistening
one sixteenth seized ends of raw thongs

you weigh the rifle you watch every inch
along fields ancient corn plants rivers
ravines New Spain traces Tenochtitlan's terrain

your blanket spreads over

attracted the gold silence through which
through which water spreads over
how when groups of the first Spaniards
in America searching

the ore in the night air they destroy
your whitish bones bright red stems mark
mark the corpse gouged with cries of

insane forest land sea-water intones conquests
searching America the groups of Spaniards
destroy your whitish bones now ore
now ore exceeds its value how under their
clothing soaking cell by cell

dark faults nitric acids so that the Spaniards
slash your armpits gouged letters New Spain
sunlight in the holes a string of little

a string of little skulls

you take upon your lap blankets there along
the edge plague spreads over you watch
mounted riders folding their arms

tightly twisted around his body raw thongs
her head eyes covered she passes her hands
their attention tracks faults

traces Tenochtitlan's terrain

letters segment one for the crow one
for the cutworm

then as she voyages took
took delicate blossoms deviates
from a sixteenth of one

then taking it upon her lap blankets
infected with plague her forearm
tightens spreads over

a cold molecular cloud seeding

sinking through silt ash silt clay

hydrogen helium chalk moves animal
outlines Mona voyages

all over America took delicate blossoms

scattered as leaves sweeten then
you looked at a circular house
Salia's impudent mouth eating buttons

then she looked at a circular house
saw Salia blowing black dust

he scattered delicate blossoms
cramped his wrist cutting

disgorges dark green routes

through which water runs spreads over

America

invades the body breaks swells scraps of
parchment triples the arms of the cross

ice walls diagonal lines strips of bark
wandering east to west point of pulsation
nearer and nearer gather sap and resin
extract

you lower your wrist plagued by doubt

doubt giving shock and wonder there in
a wood your attention tracks dry black
paint

his jaw falls open the hands and feet
positioned correctly rigid surgical
slashes parchment fused

days of the Aztec calendar cross expose
circular sides rifles against the walls
you mistrust

my wrist dark ridge of seam hardness
of surgical scar vivifying

she passes the death cart loaded with
loaded with scraps of metal

Spaniards wearing braided silk belts
Florida through which blood jets
ancient corn plants shadowed upside-down
a cooking cauldron

the horizon falls off in flesh smells

the paste of corn pushing
she drew the body of hair and water
after a few years the Spaniards

crossed origins when the Spaniards
invaded the land your breasts opening
lactarious she voyages all over America

over prairies and forests streams and desert
interwoven raw thongs his speech was
changed burned their speech until
your mouth nearer and nearer

their mouths smell of paste of corn
incantations moving

so that the Spaniards seized the gold
walls drawn in black paint Leo na r do
yours are all the tribes your attention
tracks dry black paint

you mistrust lines of letters days of
the Aztec calendar how when groups of
the first Spaniards

gold attracted the gold sea-water dark
scrotal sacs

the ore in Tlascala how under corn plants
slashed skin water covers

she faults the drawing became the corpse
along ruin and defeat the legend pulsates
large and small mountains burning

then stripped you saw faults tremble
the bright patterns along the red halves
how when the Spaniards set fire

set fire armed like us the owl and wildcats
nearer and nearer wind made of stone
while she soaks a blanket her wrist cramps

cursing the place fixed and raised his
and raised his hands smeared with red paint
skull and ear veined scrotal sac

how when you are reading a paper about
rivers ravines defeat

spreads over lodges in ear and skull
grains flakes she scattered upon her lap
delicate blossoms through her lips

through her lips black dust seeding

sinking through silt ash silt clay your
attention tracks the first Spaniards
drawn in black paint they stare down

they stare down from white walls
dark ridged hands and feet dark ridged
cuts your tongue pulsates lines of letters

lines of letters of penance blowing
black dust

where your leather soldiers point
the beginning

sketch diagonal lines massive groups
of christians folding their arms standing
each stroke notched stick black dust
your neck stretches Mictlantecuhtli

he who makes pus

broken rocks near a forked tree
spirals white glow patterns crops of corn
she passes wearing dark gold sandals
a circle of blood congeals

plants from her hands floating like
floating like props mortar used moving
the head and torso elbows face cut
into glass

who were there first deliver up all

raw gouged letters

yellow corn and of white corn they made
their flesh spreads over a burning cross
black hands one by one

write their names bright red halves
of a circular house
they stare down from white walls
cuts darkening the parchment

hardened letters of the unnamed island
when Leo na r do was forty outlines
of the first voyage

five hundred turns Flora counting
fifty-six Columbus's first voyage

who were there first deliver up all
beginning with a loaf of wax
imprints of hardened letters

they saw a great fire come out of come
out of the mountains

Before the foot knows how to walk
it moves towards death

crows their claws searching
many men and many women came each bringing
something for the Spaniards

Salia sketches a burning cross
And some of them paint their faces
all is past you know

all over America a cold molecular fire
until you found the Indies many flying
fish flew into the ship

Mona draws burns from a notched stick

In the same month Jews from all your
from all your Dominions were expelled

covers the water raw gouged letters

asked by signs if we came peacefully
and from the east

with weight of hardened letters
New Spain when letters of the unnamed
island burns from

burns from a notched stick your leather
soldiers floating like props spices
filled casks dark ridge

inflames angled letters cracks
in the white walls

then birds pumas gold leaf kept your
eyes intently fixed your attention
tracks the first Indians many men

and many women came some of them
paint their faces

under a diseased wood pools reflecting
a knife stuck into your
into your whitish bones now ore
nor ore exceeds its value

you take soil so that close right
to left from end to end toward the sun
boundaries shadowing

Indian and white a string of little

a string of little skulls

invaded the land they took sides
correctly positioned walls measured

the skulls of different origins you

watch spilling corn right to left over
New Spain black paint blisters

Flora pauses weighs ancient corn plants
metallic state dust dead patterns
hardened letters America

mark tracks in black paint a few years

snakes vomited the Spaniards we leave
our bones in moist soil slipping
slipping a photograph under the vines
one by one

letters gouged in the parchment
she takes upon her lap rings gloves
his mouth fills with spittle Salia
sketches a burning cross

in moist clumps of earth imprints of
each stroke raw gouged letters

who were there first deliver up all

symbols of my being ground their bones
first they made their flesh according
to the legend

they took squares of purple velvet
Indian and white a string of little

a string of little skulls

Searching America

they took squares of purple velvet making
a sixteenth of one
Indian and white a string of little

a string of little skulls broken resin
in the hands dust of Aztec names
then as she voyages she looks at a circular
house
infected with plague her hard muscle bears
the weight every inch of white walls
lit sloping sinking through silt ash silt
clay

you add here a little story Sigmund reflects

attracted exploration and conquests
searching America the first Spaniards

then as they voyage took delicate
blossoms deviates hardens flesh and bones

as leaves sweeten cast lots with a handful
her wrist cramped cutting along fields
tightens strings of silk

image of seams through which blood jets
Flora voyages then she looked at a circular
house saw Salia blowing black dust

clay silt ash silt where they built houses

placing near a forked tree your blanket
days of the Aztec calendar

you are waiting increase and glory
only Catholic Christians you say

you say the increase and glory how much
more so for Spain no foreigner set foot
set foot or trade here for

the boundaries limits of these unnamed
these unnamed islands deep pink and some
of the people know nothing

the people know nothing about weapons
center desire and delight Spaniards halt
wearing braided silk belts

their bodies through which blood jets
the Spaniards smelling the flesh
slashed skin water covers

there was an island that was all gold
a few years snakes opening your speech
to their tongue you take a knife and stab

stab end to end asked by signs where stones
are found with gold-colored spots gold leaf
fills their mouths the Spaniards

who were there first deliver up all

saw many of the people like the others
naked and painted some of them

some of them with white symbols some with
some with red some with black

center the cross end to end fainter

fainter and fainter lines diagonal
halt Spaniards wearing braided silk
belts their bodies pulsation scrotal

so that they seized the gold but that
all is past you know
your breasts and your iron-gray braids

and your armpits opening you see
hydrochloric nitric acids quartz veins
circling white gold exposes deep pink
seams through which blood jets

floating like props notched sticks
sinking through silt ash silt clay
smelling the flesh the Spaniards
scrotal sacs blowing black dust

you came upon Indian tracks through

through fear three long strokes
offering your long gray hands cast
cast lots with a handful of corn
burns from a notched stick you ride

you ride up close probed and seethed
left to right multiplied there in
the East

all over America a cold molecular fire

covers the water dark gold letters
days of the Aztec calendar slashes

her description how when you are reading
a paper about rivers ravines defeat

he stares down from white walls dark ridged
lines of letters of penance cramps
cramps your wrist your attention tracks

raw gouged letters

who were there first deliver up all
she sees human figures you mistrust the quest
for gold you doubt earth red marked

a stream of molten lava burning

broken rocks near a forked tree
one by one many men and many women came
each bringing something
massive groups of christians folding

folding their arms standing
point lines of soldiers each stretches
his neck broken patterns of blood

floating like props glass cut
until you found the Indies signs
of burns from a notched stick

Mona says that the harbor of Mares is
among the best in the world
lines of letters of penance blowing
black dust

that the harbor of Mares has the best breezes
and the most gentle people

all painted many Spaniards their necks
stretch swell

Flora gave them blue the paste of corn
your being ground received so that

so that Spaniards seized the gold

ship all new flow tampered all new
dehydrated a warm dry wind that blows for days
cracks among other blanks Mona mistrusts
your quest

she went to look at the dead lying
lying who were there first there out from
a mass of surgical scar defeat

defeat as big as a hand and dredging until

so that they seized the gold know unnamed

she says that the harbor of Mares she found
has the most gentle people
bringing gold and cloth salt and slaves

a mass underground lovingly a gift

a gift reddish-yellow used for coinage
and jewelry wounds with the fat from
the corpse stripped

stripped the corpse extracted the gold
a warm dry wind that blows for days

doubt you mistrust the quest for gold
extracted marked with a piece of red earth
green gold an alloy of gold

her jaw falls open

they are very gentle and do not know
what evil is nor do they kill others
nor steal

Flora pauses weighs ancient corn plants

as a stream of molten lava from a volcano
burns she passes the death cart loaded with
loaded with scraps of metal
that island a cold molecular fire

increase and glory triples the arms
of the cross black paint slashes
days of the Aztec calendar your armpits

your armpits opening exposes deep pink
sheets of gold leaf a mass of surgical
scar a few feet of soil under

under your mouth nearer and nearer
through fear floating like props
notched sticks in moist soil walls
sinking

many flying fish flew into the ship
when the unnamed island sends up shoots

shoots that feed under a diseased wood
your whitish bones

many flying fish flew into the ship

lines of christians waiting a string
a string of little skulls

it grows here on the unnamed island when
events before

Before the foot knows how to walk it moves
towards death
you departed Friday the third day of August
of the year 1492 when you were forty-one
counting five hundred turns

who were there traded for much gold
projected out from the island of naked
people you saw

you saw a great fire come out of
large and small mountains across the
waters dividing cords of veins

the quest for gold lash-like sutures
raw gouged letters spelling New Spain
where massive groups halt

Spaniards halt wearing braided silk
belts grains flakes nuggets
then as they voyage took a burning cross

gouged ancient corn plants her bones
in moist soil

so that they seized the gold
but that all is past you know

they prized your cape of fine red color
our mouths nearer and nearer incantations
moving

and the stem which is close to the root
veined dark ridged smell the paste
smell the paste of corn how letters

days of the Aztec calendar how when groups
set fire time began to weigh
five hundred turns Flora counting

Flora counting fifty-six Columbus's
first voyage

island of outlines fills in this blank
horizon then you became

you became the chronicler of defeat
spreads over stripped the corpse extracted
the gold

moisture oxygen they stare down from
a mass of surgical scar her whitish bones
dust grains flakes of salt

what evil is burns dark ridge there
was an island that island unnamed
larger than England increase swells

with weight of hardened letters these
unnamed rivers ravines spiral marked
marked with a piece of red earth

the harbor of Mares has the best breezes

they had a piece as big as a hand and
of other metals dredging until you

until you found the Indies signs you
are reading lines of letters

lines of letters of penance each bringing
a notched stick gouged ancient corn plants
swell hardness of surgical scar

his eyes mistrust the waters but that
the harbor of Mares has the best breezes
and the most gentle people

mass cordlike disease you are reading
a paper about data for the quest for gold
know that in defeat ravines a warm dry

a warm dry wind that blows for days

fills in this blank
then she became the chronicler there

there was an island that island unnamed
floating like props glass cut into human
figures you see human figures my attention

tracks metals in veins burning lava
she says that the harbor of Mares
she found has the most gentle people

the most gentle people bringing something

he guesses how disease spreads over stripped

stripped the corpse extracted the gold

I doubt you mistrust my quest through
the lines opening stone and mortar center

center desire and delight there was an island
that was all gold

the boundaries limits of your being your
mouth fills with spittle hardened black
paint no foreigner set foot set foot or
trade here for hardness of surgical scar

know that in defeat ravines a warm dry
a warm dry wind that blows for days

who were there first deliver up all

for you took squares of purple velvet they were
weakened by disease spreading over all

disease spreading over all the land
sketches a notched stick she describes

she describes the punishment with fire

with fire and blood came Spaniards halt
you came upon Indian tracks you guess you are
reading lines of letters

there was an island that island unnamed
floating like props glass cut into human
figures you see human figures

stripped the corpse extracted the gold
your wrist cramps dredging opening

opening cracks

water from drum drunk you feel that
your return from

the first voyage where your leather
soldiers stick in the mouth symbols
of your being ground under our feet

that island larger than England by signs
point to massive groups darkening

eyes intently fixed on the soil so that
cracks in the white walls
who were there first deliver up all

you left nets and hooks moving hooks
dragging a burning cross half of their
names spelled the unnamed island

that island a cold molecular fire
burns from a notched stick Spaniards
stretch their necks right to left
windpipes filling

so that they seized the gold but that
the third day of August on Friday
your sketch folds each part slashed

Mictlantecuhtli he who makes pus

your sketch slashed lines diagonal
each stroke raw gouged letters a string

a string of little skulls

READING A PAPER

dredging then the third day marked
New Spain letters slipping through

through fear three long strokes they
describe how when you are reading a paper
burns you see human figures one by one
who were there first deliver up all

the lines opening hydrochloric nitric
acids quartz veins dissolving

dissolving her hard muscle infected
with plague smell the burns their hair
cut off halt Spaniards came

she came upon Indian tracks she guesses
how disease spreads time began to weigh
five hundred turns Flora counting

lines of letters of penance then she

she became the chronicler there was an
island floating

that the harbor of Mares has the best breezes
and the most gentle people

give an account of all that had happened
how when you are reading a paper about rivers
ravines defeat

Mictlantecuhtli he who makes pus

filling scrotal sacs a string
a string of little skulls cracks filled
clay silt ash silt

she is reading about the quest for gold
dissolving her hard muscle burns counting

counting infected letters spelling New Spain
soil burns with plague smell the hair cut off
than the stomach brain dark blotches

days of the Aztec calendar a string
a string of little skulls she rubs her wrist
marked with a piece of red earth
you drink water from drum drunk you feel

you feel that your return from the first
voyage in the same month Jews from all

Jews from all your dominions were expelled
Spaniards halt wearing braided silk belts
grains flakes nuggets writing you saw

you saw a great fire you describe

you describe the punishment with fire

But the bench which they offered you
was of hot stone

through mistrust the lines of letters
center desire and delight there was an island
that was all gold stripped the corpse
hardness of surgical scar

they killed some of them with white
symbols some with red some with black

your attention spans species of plants

floating

she said that you are in that center
center desire and delight there was an island
that was all gold
seen on a chart you doubt the boundaries

through these lines of letters you saw
you saw fire and blood you feel your return
from the first voyage

you left nets and hooks moving hooks
stick in the mouth through the lines opening

he answers a question about the island
because you mistrust reading lines of letters
there was an island that island unnamed
floating like props

she came upon Indian tracks counting
counting paths and places for days
for days a warm dry wind know that defeat
has come

disease fills dark ridged blisters you
look at a circular house your attention
fills in the blank stare you are reading
a paper about data

stripped the corpse extracted the gold
her hard muscle marked with a piece
of red earth

more than growth of yellow corn
and of white corn day-by-day he

he is tainted his doubt severs lines
of letters seen on a chart your desire
and delight in their rings braided silk
belts

they said to us keep on playing the flute
and singing and painting and carving
you are reading about the quest

about the quest for gold these unnamed
these unnamed rivers ravines outlines
as big as a hand spreads over stripped

stripped methodical their quest
know that in defeat the search for water
filling her hands are raised

she says that the harbor of Mares
she found has the most gentle people

you see human figures stretch their necks
right to left force of her being they
would give her a share the weight
of red earth

you are reading lines of letters a mass
of nets and hooks then the stomach brain
blood cells in this folds each part

that island a cold molecular fire

you discover day-by-day you drew the skulls

that he feels the skin of the drum
each beat severs their names you doubt
ground under rising yellow corn
diagonal methodical more than

your desire and delight of letters seen
on a chart she discovers a notched stick
she drew the skulls then the stomach

then the stomach brain blood cells
that water from drum drunk filling soil
tainted Mictlantecuhtli he who makes pus

a string of little skulls drawn with

black chalk

each stroke delivers up all day-by-day
burns yellow skin layers your sketch
a cold molecular fire

descriptions you are reading filling
cracks in the white walls in human figures
share the weight massive groups
Spaniards darkening

spelled the unnamed island

when she asked them she was told that
the islands had always been there

day-by-day hands sever your description
their rings braided silk belts

we said to them keep on playing the flute
and singing and painting and carving

they painted all the letters blue
a mass multiplied groups of christians

you permit us to fall into a snare
I am giving a description you are reading
lines of letters

letters of penance blowing black dust
her skin reddish-yellow used for coinage
and jewelry tastes like the paste of corn

like the paste of corn to our Spanish
palates we remind you of grass pushing
through opening cracks red dots grow
into holes for days disease fills

disease fills the scrotal sacs lodges
in ear and skull marked with a piece
of red earth as a stream of molten lava
spreads over

there was an island that was all gold

she is giving a gift you mistrust her
desire and delight his wrist cramps
extracted the gold white gold exposes

exposes deep pink seams punctured her
ears and her arms

so that they seized the gold

caught the people on the roads some
of them with white symbols some with red
some with black

how when you are reading a paper about
defeat has come find disease fills

disease fills dark ridged slowly as silt
the weight every inch opens a stream of molten
lava burning for days glass cut

glass cut into human figures she sees
human figures red dots grow into holes
a warm dry wind that blows for days fills
in this blank

her attention spans species of plants floating

floating like props know that in defeat
there was an island that island unnamed
floating like props there was an island
that was all gold

their wrists marked with a piece of red earth
they rubbed skulls he watches black paint
blister weighs hardened letters America

she faults the drawing slices letters
New Spain describes how when she is reading
a paper burns she sees her hard muscle
deep pink

alone they killed some of them with white
symbols some with red some with black

black paint blisters crisis opens strips
bones above black soil

above black soil head and torso increase
and glory mouths of Spaniards filled

filled with angled letters their jaws
push under the gold walls only increase
swells under a few feet

under a few feet of soil ancient corn plants
dark ridge there was an island that was
all gold limits nothing as a stream

as a stream of molten lava from a volcano

hardness of surgical scar rigid these unnamed
these unnamed rivers ravines

lava spreads over lodges in ear and skull
she faults the drawing you became the corpse
along ruin and defeat
defeat strips strips the ancient corn plants

and Columbus raised his hands marked

marked with a piece of red earth
no foreigner set foot set foot or trade here

only Catholic Christians some of them
some of them with white symbols some with
red some with black imprints

black imprints of hardened letters
outlines of the first voyage
In the same month Jews from all your Dominions
were expelled

it had all been defeat her doubt
day-by-day usefully draws comparisons
gold has been known

gold has been known from prehistoric times
engraved their pictures you took a notched
stick your attention drifting

severing human figures tenth day of
the Aztec calendar blanks fill

blanks fill with fire

But a mass of tendrils harden his mouth
fills with spittle she pauses sketches
she pauses sketches a burning cross

of yellow corn and of white corn they
made their flesh water from drum drunk
she feels that your return from

that island marked New Spain you are
reading the beginning little story
reflects Sigmund

Flora printed all the letters blue
her wrist cramps she answers a question
we mistrust a paper about data

these are the names a thousand and one
times you are reading a warm dry wind
that blows for days

clay silt ash silt

this year you doubt day-by-day

made their figures into monumental bronze
in the wildness of the scene you are reading
the beginning little story your attention

fixes on red earth you reflect on the sketch
of a woman on horseback her blanket wrapped
around her waist through a mass

a mass of forms and colors fill with fire
that burns for days a warm dry wind
it drifts through nets and hooks weaves
strings of muscle metallic state

her doubt imprints your attention suckles
naked hills there was an island that island
center desire that island marked New Spain
that pictures you took

you took a burning cross entered the edge
your mouth blowing dust dead patterns
probing raw gouged letters your return
that island

that island would not exist reddish-
yellow pushing through

a thousand and one times blanks fill

blanks fill hurled them I threw the skulls
of the dead

his wrist cramps he pauses

all the mountains were full of pines
your attention drifting you took
you took this route she saw

severing human figures a question
as a stream of lava hardens
imprints some of them with white
open bones fragment raw sutures

fragment raw sutures day-by-day reading
the beginning little story being the season
their attention drifting nets

the stomach brain blood cells day-by-day

she feels the skin of the drum each beat
methodical he draws letters seen on
letters seen on a chart that each beat
severs their names

      so I hope in our lord
      order to bring to the king
      your kingdoms in a tranquil
      state free of heresy and evil

and to go to the southeast to seek gold
and spices

spelled the unnamed island a string
a string of little skulls drawn with

black chalk

increase your doubt forms that island
you calculated

she sights the territory you discover
you are drawing skulls water filling up

sunk under the weight you increase
your doubt ground black chalk Mona's

Mona's long gray hands her wrists move
like a weaver opening light shone
light shone reddish-yellow you see

human figures that they feel the skin
of the drum blood cells desire opening
their breasts

you heard their voices you are reading
lines scent of the hunter
we said to them keep on playing the flute
and singing and painting and carving

mistrust imprints of hardened letters
a question painted in blue she sees gold
and spices a reddish-yellow deer skin

head and torso bits of wire a mass
a mass of nets and hooks seen on a chart

made a curve toward that island marked
New Spain she pauses fills in the sketch

you are seated on horseback ride up to stone
walls then you feel
desire and delight force in the flint

so that they seized the gold

THERE WAS AN ISLAND THAT WAS ALL GOLD

last walk on earth after Spaniards

in an iron cage opening with fire and blood
halt Spaniards halt

describe cracks opening

moved right to left you permit her to fall
into a snare empty like a weaver marks
darkening layers day-by-day she nets and hooks

he seeks the fault you hear the sound
of the flute in ear and skull disease fills
the scrotal sac

aim their thrusts there was an island that
was all gold caught the people
always following made a curve we heard
the horsemen ordering you to brand

wiped three wounds one in the thigh one
in the head one in her left arm the same curve
close a stretch of skin desire and delight

you stare down reading skin flayed he
orders you to brand human figures fill with
fill your attention suckles

Leo na r do had not heard you you answer
correctly you calculate the edge reflect
reflect on the sketch

of Indian women

you are hearing why you have come

these things happened we gave maize you
are those whom our ancestors her wrists
move like a weaver she pauses

it appears on skin the angled letters group
fill with fire raw gouged letters

all the mountains were full of pines
my attention drifting spans species of plants
we are those who draw lines on a chart

desire of letters burned

her attention drifting blood cells he marks
that island

nothingness that pictures you are seeing
Spaniards projected backwards your eyes
on the ceiling

reddish-yellow skin flayed you stare down
reading

we gave gold you are those whom our ancestors
took this route dissolves a mass of nets
and hooks toward that island

so that they seized the gold they said
they said to us keep on playing the flute
and singing and painting and carving

and his left arm a stretch of skin wiped
slowly three wounds

you question winding her hair molded

hills is she the corpse names
with fragments of bone you spelled New Spain
then Flora marked their breasts

earth the face of the corpse marked
marked this sign drawn with black chalk
wanted to make angled letters

where they strike them immense waves
calculated my mistrust bits of paper
mistrust hidden when there was neither

neither sky nor earth

mourned for Nahuatl the parchment you
stretch under the weight those are three
three wounds one in the thigh one
in the head and torso

two hundred if they were to hang from
the trees then the weight you missed
drifting into a snare skin yellow

the horsemen ordering you to brand
moved left to right he stares down
the passages strings of raw gouged

gouged muscles his attention suckles
keep on repeating their same
their same shouts and songs

who first by night and cut three wounds

her skull fills that island polished black
burned the houses of grass so his attention
to your answer you doubt the map of the Aztec
Nahuatl the first page

you are reading a mass whitened with chalk

times folded length of her blanket wrapped

that a thousand and one times that island
polished hieroglyphs to strike us

the one called Metztli Spaniards put
your attention drifting you took this

this surface of the earth

in the wildness of the scene hardening skin
of the drum her wrist flames all the mountains
were full of pines winds through

through human figures a question as a stream

as a stream of urine then the blood known
by the name letters like a flock of birds
polished black

toward earth hurled hardened all
all the mountains of stones only to give
a sign in chalk calculated

blanks mistrust a paper about data

day-by-day read lime and stone fragments
of the parchment she describes the parchment

mistrust day-by-day on horseback following
Mona's left arm naked changed one woman echoes
a question gold has been known then they

they stare down clothed with the light
opening where we heard voices in Spanish
keep on playing the flute and singing

and painting and carving male and female
seeks the fault widened this route naked
under the weight Spanish methodical head
and torso you group the letters curve

the half-burned stones you increase imprints
like a weaver marks darkening layers

that island was your aim taking our women
and children walk on earth imprints two
hundred Spaniards gold has been known
from prehistoric times

she describes the parchment tears seize gold
you have come and her left arm slowly
slowly three wounds you are those

whom our ancestors

gave a cake of salt desire opening their
breasts light shone reddish-yellow seeing
Spaniards then they

scooped out half-burned stones we said
you are reading lines in the flint